BEYOND *the* X's & O's *of* ATHLETIC COACHING

7KEYS
to Being a GREAT
COACH

Become Your Best and They Will Too

by: **ALLISTAIR McCAW**

7 Keys to Being a Great Coach
Become Your Best and They Will Too
Copyright © 2016 Allistair McCaw

First Edition – May 2016

ISBN: 978-0-578-17952-0

Library of Congress Cataloging-in-Publication Data:

Category: Athletic Coaching, Coach Education, Motivational

Written by: Allistair McCaw | McCawMethod@gmail.com

Edited by: Kathy Whyte

Cover Design, Text Layout by: Eli Blyden | CrunchTime Graphics

Published in the United States of America

Acknowledgements

I'd like to start by expressing my sincere gratitude and appreciation that you've decided to purchase or pick up my book — *thank you!*

Let me start by saying that I write from a coach's perspective because that is what I am. One thing I'll admit is that I am by no means an expert. I am a learner. The term 'expert' to me, kind of has a 'finished and complete' label to it. I see myself as a life long learner, and will always be an unfinished quantity.

Having been in the sports performance industry for just over two decades now, I look around me and see far more smarter people than myself. However, I've come to realize that it's not all about talent or who has the most degrees behind their name, but rather who has a desire to keep learning and nurture a passion for serving others. One of the purposes of this book is to share some of my personal experiences and thoughts of what it takes to be a great coach and why the best succeed in this field. I wanted to share with you what I have learned, what's worked for me and of course what hasn't. I have dedicated the last 20 years in finding out what makes the best coaches the best, why they succeed, and how they get the best from their athletes and teams, day in and day out.

I hope that this book provides you with some idea's and answers. I encourage you to read this book with a nice colorful and bright highlighter in hand, as I find this the best way to remember things. Anyone who has borrowed a book from me will tell you how colorful it was inside! I also hope that my book gives you the motivation to keep waking up every morning and wanting to be a better coach and person than you were the day before.

There are so many people to thank for this, in fact, too many to mention. Fellow coaches, athletes (past and present), my friends and family and of course to Maddy, who was so patient and outstanding throughout the whole process. A big thanks to Eli Blyden, for the amazing book design. Last but certainly not least, Kathy Whyte, my editor, who did a superb job.

Of course I need to extend a special thanks to all those who have influenced my career and helped me be a better coach. Coaches who maybe don't even know they have, but are pioneers in the sports performance field namely Carolyn Vorster, Michael Boyle, Mark Verstegen and Vern Gambetta amongst others.

To God, thank you for your grace and faithfulness. You have never left my side, and thank you for showing me that my ways are not always your ways.

My greatest appreciation to all those who contributed to this book in whatever way, you know who you are, and again, too many to mention. Nothing is possible without others and no worthwhile achievement is a solo act — *thank you all so much from the bottom of my heart.*

Finally, my hope is that this book will challenge and inspire you along your journey as a coach and person. I feel blessed to be able to share what I feel makes a great coach and what I've learned along the way.

If I could add one last thing, it would be this: Follow your passion, live your life to the fullest, and never, never stop believing in yourself. You have what it takes to be great! Believe it. Don't wait, because the time will never be right. Act now.

– Allistair

*The most powerful
performance factor is people. It's how you connect,
energize and inspire them.*

- Allistair McCaw

Disclaimer

Table of Contents

7 KEYS

to Being a GREAT COACH

Become Your Best and They Will Too

*Become your best,
and they will too.*

Introduction

Right now I'm probably about 33,000 feet above the Pacific Ocean as I'm travelling on an Air New Zealand flight from Auckland to Houston. I've just had an incredibly rewarding two weeks speaking at various coach conferences, as well as athlete motivation and parent workshops in Melbourne, Australia, and Auckland, New Zealand, highlighted by a quick whistle stop tour at the famous Eden Park Stadium, home of the World Rugby Cup champions, the All Blacks.

After many years of deliberating, I feel more inspired than ever to finally put pen to paper and share my thoughts, experiences, and ideas of what I feel constitutes a great coach. My goal was to write a book that kept things as simple as possible, without getting too complex, as those who know me will tell you I am more the simple coach than the scientific type. I also wanted a book with a difference, something that not only motivates other coaches to be more and reach for more, but to share some of my own experiences I've had during my journey.

Even from the very first day that I started out as an 18-year-old in the fitness industry, I was always on a mission and journey to discover what truly makes a great coach and trainer. Now, 22 years later, I feel I'm a little closer to that answer, but will happily admit that I still haven't figured it all out just yet. In fact, I probably never will, because as a lifelong learner, I am constantly on a journey to find out and discover more. That's why it's not uncommon for me to change my mind from time to time due to learning something new that makes more sense. Life never stops giving us lessons and that is the beauty and mystery of it.

I've spent the last 20 years travelling the world with the goal of finding what really makes a great coach. I've burned up air miles and visited every possible sports event I could, whether it be a World Cup rugby match, a college volleyball game, or a youth kids' soccer game. Through my many experiences as a performance coach in different sports at every possible level and age group, I have realized that there are many roads to becoming a great coach or trainer.

Another added advantage I've had in my pursuit of finding what makes a great coach, is that being a performance coach (strength/fitness/mindset), I've been able to work alongside coaches in a variety of sports, and this has enabled me to get a closer insight to what great coaching really is.

I am blessed and grateful to have been able to share meals, training runs, gyms, courts, fields, tracks, and flights with some of the brightest minds in coaching and athletic performance. I have always loved to pick their brains and learn more about their journeys and experiences.

It doesn't matter what sport, age group or level it may be, I want to observe as many coaches, players, and parents as possible, and simply learn as much as I can. In fact, just in the past month I've attended a U.S. badminton team practice, a swimming meet, tennis at the Australian Open in Melbourne, a Cricket International match at the Melbourne Cricket Ground (MCG), a soccer match between Auckland City and Wellington Phoenix, as well as a junior high baseball game in Tampa, Florida. Each time I come away from a sports event, I feel I have learned something new and valuable that I can take with me.

It's an ongoing classroom of lessons and experiences. I have discovered that coaching a sport is not about the sport itself, but rather it's more about people, and getting the best out of them. It's about helping them discover that what they thought might not have been possible, actually is.

When one thinks of the word 'experience' we automatically think of time or years spent doing something. However, there's a big difference between having 20 years of experience in one area and having 20 years of experience in multiple endeavours. Therefore, a crucial goal of mine is to become focused on all of life's experiences so that I have more to offer the athlete, coach, or parent as we work together.

If I had to look at the top coaches or trainers in the S & C world (Strength & Conditioning), my guess is I wouldn't rank anywhere in the top 95 percent of impressive educational backgrounds or qualifications, as there are a plethora of smarter coaches and trainers out there. But, I can say that I would rank within the top 5 percent of the hardest working coaches, utilizing my opportunities and determination. This is a message I especially want to impress on young trainers and coaches: your attitude and work ethic will get you further than your education or certifications. That's not to say you shouldn't get the best education possible, but realize that it is only your entry ticket.

My work experiences have not been exclusive to the coaching or training world. They started with delivering newspapers as a 10-

year-old, and progressed to flipping burgers, cleaning gym restrooms, working behind the counter at the squash courts, working as a mascot for a soft drink company, selling light bulbs and fittings, waiting tables at restaurants, working as a volunteer for animal shelters and managing gyms.

Without knowing it, through these numerous work experiences, I was given an insight into being accountable, staying disciplined, working with people in a team environment, and knowing what it means to earn and spend a dollar. Little did I know where these experiences would take me one day!

I was always driven to succeed. From the age of around 9, my dream was to become a professional tennis player. At 14, I took up running and then the sport of Duathlon (running and biking). I would go on to represent my country five times at the World Championships, spend a few years racing and competing in Europe and winning two national titles. Today my mindset hasn't changed much, but I admit that it has diverted me from wanting to be the best, to wanting to bring out the best in myself. It's a standard I try live up to each day.

Today, this is the lesson I pass on to those I coach or mentor, whether athletes, parents, or coaches. It's all about doing your best with what you've got and 'controlling the controllables'. You can't control being the best there is, you can't control outcomes, rankings or ratings, but you can definitely control the ability to bring the best out in yourself. Setting high standards, bringing energy to the moment, and the daily process of doing your very best each day are what count the most in my books.

Last, but not least, I believe that every great coach leaves a legacy. When it comes to what legacy I would love to leave one day, it's pretty simple: that I was able to help others believe what they thought wasn't possible, is possible; and that I helped instill good values, standards, and principles to those I coached and trained.

Trophies and medals rust, but being able to influence and change a person's life for the better through sport is the best reward I can possibly think of as a coach.

What legacy will you leave?

Committed to your Success,

Allistair McCaw,
Somewhere above the Pacific Ocean
27th January, 2016

"A good coach can change a game.
A great coach can change a life".

\- John Wooden

CHAPTER 1

Standards

"It all starts with your standards."

\- Allistair McCaw

In the coaching world, I believe you will be defined by two things: the legacy you leave behind and the standards you keep as a coach and human being. When I think of these two things, my mind automatically goes to people like the legendary basketball coach John Wooden, or former Manchester United football manager Sir Alex Ferguson. It's true what they say that the standards you set are the standards and results you get. Standards are a foundation that are far superior to rules, they define morally correct and acceptable behaviours. Standards are guidelines to live by and to hold each other accountable.

The standards you choose are central to how you will define your career and how your athletes will best remember you. These standards are the foundation of your program, a quality seal you put on your product, and that product is you. And it's you who gets to decide those standards.

There are three kinds of standards coaches should set:

1. Personal standards

2. Standards within their organization / academy / club / team

3. Standards for their athletes and clients (those they coach or train)

1. Personal Standards

When I look back to my childhood days, the coaches and teachers I best remember are not those who were the trophy or championship hunters, but rather those who cared about me as a person and taught life lessons. They didn't focus on just athletic skills, drills, or tactics. I best remember the ones who were strict and held me accountable, but were always fair, and at times, good fun.

What I liked about these type of coaches and teachers is that I always knew where I stood, and I knew where the boundaries lay. The practices were always fun, but tough, and they taught me about the importance of effort, attitude, teamwork and responsibility. High standards and discipline were the order of the day.

I'm now into my 22nd year of being a coach and trainer, and I have always been driven to find out what really makes a great coach. I have discovered that to be a great coach or leader requires many factors and attributes. For example: a vast experience in the field you are working in, a sound knowledge, a good work ethic, as well as good communication and people skills.

My quest from day one has been to discover what it really takes to get the best out of people and help them realize what they thought was impossible, is possible, because to me, that is what real coaching is all about.

Coaching to me is about people. It's about taking them to levels they didn't even think were possible.

I believe to be a great coach or leader, it all starts with who you are and the way you choose to live your life. Your personal beliefs, values, principles, habits, and daily routines determine who you eventually become.

Great coaches have great people skills.

If we look back through history, we discover that the great coaches who are best remembered are those who had a deeper understanding of the person, not only the sport, people like UCLA basketball great John Wooden, the 49ers' coach Bill Walsh, and more recently, football coach Pep Guardiola, coach of European powerhouse teams such as Barcelona and Bayern Munich.

In my two decades as a performance coach and trainer, I've had the privilege to work alongside some of the world's best coaches in a variety of sports, including rugby, tennis, hockey, cricket, squash, track and field, and more. I noticed that they all have 'skills,' whether they are technical, tactical, people, etc., and they all have a substantial amount of knowledge. Some are extraordinary motivators, like tennis coaching legend Nick Bollettieri (coach to no less than 10 world no. 1 players and numerous grand slam champions, like Mary Pierce and Monica Seles). And some are exceptional educators and communicators, like the late Bob Woolmer, cricket coach of South Africa, Pakistan and Warwickshire.

However, not all great coaches 'have it all.' In fact nobody has it all. All these great coaches have their strengths and weaknesses, just like the rest of us. Sometimes coaches try to take on everything and then they ultimately fail. One thing I've learned is that you can't be everything to everyone. My philosophy is to focus on your strengths, zoom into them, and work on them every day. Moreover, coaches who have left a lasting impression on me are the ones who had high standards, not just for their teams or athletes, but for themselves. They led by example.

As a coach, you can't be everything to everyone. My philosophy is to focus on your strengths, zoom into them, and work on them every day.

These coaches exuded extremely high standards in all areas of their lives. Words like *integrity, trust,* and *honesty* came to mind when their athletes, or those who knew them, would speak about them in later years.

You see, even though the championship medals and titles go into the record books and archives, it's your values, principles, and beliefs that you'll best be remembered for as a coach or teacher. It will be these characteristics and traits that drive and steer the way you live your life and lead others. This, I believe, is where your real legacy will be remembered.

Having high standards translates to professionalism. To me the word *professional* doesn't relate to a status or level you coach, or your playing ability. In my opinion, *professional* is about your attitude, attention to details, quality of preparation, discipline, and standards. Qualities that are all 'controllables.'

As a Coach, You Need to First Set the Example.

As a coach, to demand the respect of your athletes and team, you need to first set the example. If you're the one who's telling them to be on time, work hard, and always be prepared, and you're not doing the same, then you cannot expect the trust and 'buy in' from the athlete or team. Your athletes will see your example more than hear your words.

Great coaches are best respected for who they are more than what they do. They care about others and have a deep desire to get to know the athlete better. They have an invested interest in others.

I have always believed that to be a great coach, you need to be leading a life that involves building long standing healthy relationships. Coaches should also take care of their health, like exercising and eating well. This doesn't mean they need to be following the training program or lifestyle of a professional athlete, but they should at least make an effort to stay in shape and have the energy to perform at their peak.

You see, coaching is all about energy, and if we are not taking care of ourselves as coaches from a health and wellness point of view, how can we expect to give energy to our athletes? In chapter 4, I will discuss this in more detail.

Commit yourself to the pursuit of excellence.

Personal Challenges

All my life I've been a sports and fitness fanatic. I love to set goals and challenges to keep myself focused, fired up, and fit. Back in 2013, I ran 12 marathons in 12 months in 12 different cities across the globe. This was a personal goal, one that I knew would be a tough challenge. I had to navigate and schedule my time for training in between a crazy work and travel schedule around the world. I recorded over 90 flights that year and visited 21 countries. I remember getting up at 3 a.m. in Montreal, Canada to run a marathon on my own before a scheduled 9 a.m. practice with the athlete I was working with at the time, Australian Davis Cup player, Bernard Tomic. No excuses, it had to be done that early, as working on the professional tour as a coach, you never know how the rest of the day is going to pan out.

To expect more of others,
you first have to expect more of yourself.

In 2015, I decided to run seven marathons in seven weeks, with a half marathon in between each week — a tough challenge. One of the main reasons I did this was to experiment with recovery techniques. During those seven weeks, I used cryotherapy tanks, ice baths, roller sticks, foam rolling, Epsom salt baths, hot/cold treatment, you name it. I wanted to see what worked best for the recovery of the athletes I train. I love these kinds of challenges, because it not only benefits my athletes, but also reveals how far I can push my own limits. I want to show my athletes that I am willing to put myself out there and do anything I am asking of them.

Now again, don't get me wrong. This doesn't mean you need to set some crazy goal or climb Mount Everest to obtain the respect of your athletes, but it's the effort and time you are putting into yourself that count most! Even a 5k fun run, a ride for charity, or getting into the gym a few times a week is a good enough example.

Coaches, don't underestimate the power and influence you have in performing the smallest things that require effort, even that 20 minutes in the morning you spend stretching or working out. Your athletes see this. It's more about getting out of your own comfort zone, if that's what you are asking your athletes to do. We need to remember that leaders always go first. They don't push others, but rather show them the way through their own actions and beliefs. It's about setting your personal standards in health and taking care of yourself.

It's about setting your personal standards in health and taking care of yourself.

Another standard includes our appearance — our dress code and the way we present ourselves. Do we look clean, neat, and take pride in our appearance? Are our clothes neatly pressed, shirts tucked in, and hair combed? Again these are our personal standards.

For example, a trainer or coach who wears a vest or hat backwards while he trains a client or athlete is difficult to take seriously — even worse — outdoors with a shirt off! He might be experienced and have all the knowledge in the world, but that is not the standard of a professional, in my opinion.

What about our attitude? If we are demanding a great attitude from our athletes or team members, that means our attitude as a coach needs to fit that bill too. What about our work ethic? If we expect our athletes to put in the extra work, are we doing the same as coaches in our profession?

Become your best and they will too.

What about profanity? If we use it, but then don't allow our athletes or team members to curse or swear, isn't that contradictory?

What about the way we conduct our practice sessions? Do we sit on the bench, lean up against the wall, sit on machines in the gym, or are we up and fully engaged?

What about time management? Do we demand that our athletes be there on time, but we sometimes arrive late?

Do we look professional, act professional and perform in a professional manner? These are all things that contribute to our personal standards. These standards may seem trivial to you, but they all add up and change the environment and the results at the end of the day.

That's why developing great habits and routines are important for raising your personal standards in your life style. I believe that setting standards is more than setting goals. Don't get me wrong, I do set goals, but in the book, *Burn Your Goals,* authors Joshua Metcalf and Jamie Gilbert explain that goals are in the distance and sometimes seem unreachable, whereas standards are your everyday process to becoming better. I very much believe in a process mindset and approach, as I aim to achieve my daily routines I have set for the day.

When you take care of the process (your daily routines and habits), the end results will take care of themselves.

Your standards are more important than your goals.

Life long Learners

Another common trait of great coaches is that they invest in themselves every day. They are life long learners, wanting to learn and increase their knowledge capacity as much as possible. I first learned about this from Michael Boyle, a fantastic strength coach based in Boston. Michael has worked with the Boston Bruins and the New England Patriots, among other great athletes and teams. Life long learners and great coaches love to read, attend workshops and coaching seminars, listen to podcasts, and are always researching. They understand that to better their athletes and the people around them, they need to improve themselves daily. Life long learners also associate and build relationships with other lifelong learners. I explain this in more detail in Chapter 7.

You will find that great coaches and successful people have similar daily routines and habits. For example, they get up early, they prepare for the day ahead of time, they have priorities and address those first. They take care of their health and nutrition. They nurture relationships, especially family, and are constantly looking out for others.

While on a morning run in Melbourne, Australia this year with Magnus Norman, a good friend and coach to Grand Slam winner Stan Wawrinka, Magnus spoke about the importance of coaches taking care of what really matters most: ourselves, our families, and our relationships. He put it so well by saying that, *"We need to put on our oxygen masks first before helping others,"* like the way the airline attendants give us instructions before taking off on a flight.

To be a great coach we need to be authentic. We cannot be respected and trusted if we are demanding high standards from those around us, and we don't have high standards for ourselves. I can't expect an athlete to listen to me talk about the importance of nutrition while I am standing there with a cheeseburger in my hand. As coaches, our actions are always being watched, and our attitudes are always being assessed.

I can't expect an athlete to listen to me talk about the importance of nutrition
while I am standing there with a cheeseburger in my hand.

Our personal standards are our foundation, and we need to remember that our reputation enters the room before we do. Remember that your example is more powerful than your words.

Your athletes will see your example,
more than hear your words.

My Personal Daily Routines and Standards

Since I have had a routine and structure to my day, I feel I get so much more accomplished. Developing habits and routines to my day has given me much more success in my daily activities and I feel my energy is better maintained. Having routines makes it easier to plan my day's and week's. By having these, it helps me maintain the standards I have initially set for myself.

I'm an avid reader and can sometimes finish a book within a week. I make it a habit to order two books a month from Amazon.com, but most of the time I end up ordering more. I also listen to podcasts while I train in the gym or when I run, which is how I came up with the term *'Learun'* — word play on *learning* and *running* (more about that later). In fact, of the seven marathons in seven weeks I accomplished back in November and December of 2015, I probably listened to over 20 hours of podcasts. I was able to kill two birds with one stone — get fit and learn at the same time.

I believe that structure is so important to a person's day, taking care of the priorities first, and then the rest follows. Each day I also need to achieve what I call the *4 x 20s*. I believe that no matter where I am in the world, or how busy my day is, these 4 x 20s are possible and keep me energized and on track:

My 4 x 20's:

1. 20 minutes of stretching and foam rolling
2. 20 minutes of thoughtfulness
3. 20 minute nap
4. 20 minutes (at least!) of reading and research.

An example of a typical day for me looks like this:

5:00 a.m.	Wake up, have coffee, check Twitter
5:30 a.m.	Check emails and plan the day's priorities/things to do
6:00 a.m.	20-minute stretch and foam rolling
6:30 a.m.	Breakfast: oatmeal, strawberries, blueberries. Take supplements and vitamins.

7:00 a.m.	Thoughtfulness: sending a message to an athlete who might be competing that day, sending a message to a student taking an exam or to someone that's having a birthday, etc.
7:30 a.m.	Leave for work
8:00-11:00 a.m.	Coaching or consulting
10:00 a.m.	Protein shake
11:00 a.m.	My own personal strength routine
12:00 a.m.	Lunch, return phone calls or emails
1:00 p.m.	Nap
1:30 p.m.	Administrative work / training programs
2:45 p.m.	Protein shake
3:00-6:00 p.m.	Coach or consulting
6:00 p.m.	Training run
7:00 p.m.	Dinner
8:00 p.m.	Email correspondence
8:30 p.m.	Shower
9:00 p.m.	Reading in bed
10:00 p.m.	Bedtime

I encourage you to do the same.
Setting your personal standards is about having routines,
a structure, and a plan of action.

"Your example isn't the main thing in influencing others, it's the only thing".

– Coach Don Meyer

2. Standards within Your Organization

Setting standards within your working environment or organization can also be described as, *"This is the way we do things around here."*

There are 3 things that I feel matter most in an organization:

1. Finding the right people.

2. Building a strong culture.

3. Setting high standards.

When you look at your organization, your standards and culture should be the foundation that everything else is built upon. It's like the parable of building a house on a bed of sand instead of the rock. If you don't set standards and get the culture right first, it won't matter what you do.

Your standards and culture should be the foundation that everything else is built upon.

In my travels to numerous academies, sports organizations, and schools around the world, I have noticed there is always a strong culture of a positive environment, high standards, and level of discipline present in the most successful and well-run facilities. It takes time and effort from all involved to build on these prefaces. Creating the right environment and setting the standards starts from the top down.

Greg Popovich, head coach of the San Antonio Spurs and winner of five NBA championship rings, said: *"Success within a team or organization is all about building a culture of excellence and maintaining high standards."* This is evident in the character of the players he drafts for his organization. Having spent over 25 years at the franchise, Pop (as he is known), has built a team around strong characters and leaders. Popovich prefers to choose players with character over characters. He's a man of integrity and extremely high standards, In fact, he still has the core of his players and staff from 10 years ago — quite an incredible feat in today's fast moving world of professional sports, transfers, and evolving franchises.

> *"Success within a team or organization is all about building a culture of excellence and maintaining high standards."*
>
> - Greg Popovich (San Antonio Spurs head coach)

Another great example of maintaining high standards within an organisation is former All Blacks World Rugby Cup winning coach, Graham Henry. During an interview with Henry, he mentioned that he always put standards before personalities. I have always admired the style and way Henry has led teams and dealt with pressure and adversity. Anyone who understands how deep rugby runs in the blood of every New Zealander will know that only the highest standards will do to stay in that job and succeed. Even when the All Blacks lose a match, the result is deemed a national disaster.

Another coach who sets the standards in discipline is the England Rugby coach Eddie Jones. So exceptional are the standards demanded at a Jones training session that many players struggle to deliver what is expected of them. And he doesn't apologize for it either. In his book, *Pep Confidential,* it describes ex-Barcelona and Bayern Munich football coach, Pep Guardiola, as someone who demanded unstinting effort from his players. Nothing but the best would do, and at times his exacting standards caused friction within the group. It's in these standards that the great coaches are defined. They demand the best from those around them, and of course, themselves.

"I have always put standards before personalities."

- Graham Henry (All Blacks rugby coach)

Back in 2004, New Zealand rugby was at an all-time low. After a few disappointing performances and incidents within the team, they felt it was time for a change. They believed that the strength of the team would come from the strength of their leaders and culture. They had the playing talent, but were missing the right environment. It was then that they looked to introduce a young Richie McCaw, only 23 years of age, as their new captain and leader to play a significant role in setting new standards and driving his peers to a higher level. To do this, they had to remove some key figures and senior players from the squad. This wasn't because of form, but rather the new standards and culture they were trying to indoctrinate. And as we now know, under Richie McCaw's leadership, the All Blacks became the powerhouses of world rugby and set the standard of excellence.

No one can argue that Sir Alex Ferguson is one of the most successful football coaches and managers ever. The Manchester United boss was able to build a legacy during his time there, making the club one of the most successful sporting franchises in sport of football. Ferguson was all about standards and excellence, and was all about the culture and environment of the club. He had no problem removing negative influences within the club, regardless of status or position. In Ferguson's book, *Leading,* he mentions that before you can build a great team, you first have to build a great organization, and this takes time. Ferguson was a man who led by example, going on to say, *"I got into the habit of appearing for work before the milkman arrived."*

In the *Setting Standards* chapter of his book, he mentions that **unless you understand people, it's very hard to motivate them**. Ferguson, who retired in 2013, was in management for 38 years, winning 49 trophies, making him without a doubt, Britain's most successful football manager ever.

As a coach and sports performance consultant to various sports programs within various universities in the United States and across the globe, I have observed that the most successful ones have higher standards, better levels of discipline, and a positive environment. These successful programs usually have someone at the top who believes in building a strong culture and positive environment, who places an emphasis on values and high standards.

The most successfully run programs usually have someone at the top who believes in building a strong culture and positive environment.

Your standards and culture will always drive your program. But it takes a consistent effort from all involved to uphold these values and principles. Let it slip for just a moment and things can quickly head south. As Sir Ferguson said, ***"It takes time to build a successful organization."***

As a coach it's important to know that **your standards and discipline are determined by the worst behaviour you are willing to accept.** To run a successful program, school, club, or academy, you need to have your standards laid out and understood from day one. Standards in this context can almost be seen as a 'set of rules,' but I have always found the word *standards* to be a more acceptable and less aggressive way of defining what is accepted and what isn't.

The degree of your success and results are related to the standards you have set.

Eddie Jones, rugby coach for the England National team, is another coach who believes in creating the right environment with high standards for his players and staff. In Jones words, *"Values = behaviors,"* Jones believes in developing a culture of discipline with the rules being very clear, as well as consistent communication and a very high work ethic by all those involved. Similarly, before I start working with any group or team, I lay out the standards of how I work, what is expected of them, and what they can expect from me. To have an effective working operation, there always needs to be clarity from the word *go*.

In 2012, Sir Clive Woodward, director of sport for the British Olympic Association, drew up a list of 15 standards for the 550 athletes who were chosen to compete for Team GB in the London Olympic games. These standards included things such as responsibility, performance, unity, pride, and respect. Included in those standards were things like bedtimes, time management, and noise. This is another example of just how important setting firm standards are in a team environment, from grassroots to elite levels. At the end of this chapter you can find the standards of both these fine coaches.

Standards are a guideline and a way of telling others how things are done around here.

An example is how we communicate, both verbally and written. When we speak or disagree, we do not raise our voices, but let the other person finish, instead of interrupting. We also respect the fact that we will have differences of opinion at times.

When an email is sent out, we expect an answer within a certain time frame, even if it is a short answer, like, *"Thanks, just acknowledging I have received your e-mail, I will answer in more detail within 24 hours."* We understand that things can get busy with travel, lessons, family, etc.

My main point here is that these are the small things that save a lot of unnecessary energy and frustration due to miscommunication. Waiting days upon end for an answer is unacceptable, unfair, and in my opinion, disrespectful.

Time management is also another area that is important. If you want to run a successful academy, club, or organization, it's imperative that all the coaches and staff set the example by arriving well before time and being ready before lessons or meetings begin. Again, we need to remember that if we expect this of our athletes and team, we have to set that example first.

Dress code, neatness, and pride of the badge represent another important standard to consider. Coaches and staff need to look professional and well-represented. In my opinion, most organizations and clubs that have failed, do so because high enough standards are not being set and/or adhered to. Even when you look at other successful institutions and operations, such as the world famous Bolshoi Ballet Academy in Moscow or the Berlin Music Academy, you see a rich tradition of culture, high standards, discipline and structure.

Focus on your standards more than on opinions.

Coaching is also about controlling the emotions. In this line of work we can get very caught up in what we do, the wins and the losses and how much we care.

In a study performed by the University of Leeds and Northumbria University, it was discovered that coaches who were more focused on their own high standards and less interested in the opinions of others were significantly better at controlling feelings of anger than those who were very focused on the opinions of their performance. The results showed that coaches with high personal standards — meaning they set their own high standards and focused less on other people's evaluations — were relatively good at regulating their emotions.

Remember, our standards as coaches are being watched and assessed all the time.

"Your character is who you are, your reputation is what others think of you"

\- Coach Wooden

Parents

Last but not least, the standards set by the organization need to be relayed, explained, and agreed to by the parents of the younger athletes who are within your program. Consistent and clear communications need to be in motion.

It is important that all parties involved understand their roles from day one. For example, boundaries and standards need to be set in regard to where the parents can watch or attend practices, and how they can best facilitate their child's progress, like letting the coach be the coach, and respecting his/her authority. The premise of a successful organization involving the coaching of kids requires a 'buy in' from all involved. In my experience of consulting sports clubs, academies, and organizations, if parents are left out of the equation, things can eventually break down. When I speak at workshops I advise coaches to have a meeting with parents for at least a few minutes every four to six weeks. This keeps everyone in the loop with regard to standards and expectations. More importantly, this also gives the parents a chance to share their concerns.

Remember that one of the biggest mistakes you can make as a coach is not consistently communicating with the parents in your program.

The roles of the coach, parent, and athlete:

- The coach coaches.
- The parent supports.
- The athlete plays.

Standards should be set within an organization or academy environment for the following:

- Communication within organization (fellow coaches, staff, and athletes)
- Dress code
- Time management
- Respect
- Cleaning up — after practices, etc.

- Language
- Change rooms — cleanliness
- Personal development
- Developing the culture
- Cleanliness (of facility/staff rooms/locker rooms, etc.)
- Cell phone use during coaching and lessons
- Preparation and planning of lessons, events, and competitions
- Communication between parents and athletes
- Behavior
- Equipment
- Meetings

Remember, you cannot expect your athletes to be setting and carrying out high standards, if you as an organization, coach or leader, are not setting that example first.

In a lot of programs, the Xs & Os are usually well explained and documented, but the standards are often either overlooked or forgotten.

3. Standards for the Athlete

Standards provide athletes with responsibility and holds them accountable. It's a way for them to feel a part of the process, and at the same time, contribute to a positive environment.

Much like the standards for the coaches and staff, it is vital for any successful program to have a set of standards in place for the athlete. In other words, what is acceptable and what isn't; what is tolerated and what isn't; what is expected and how he/she can contribute to the culture and environment of the team or organization.

Many teams or organizations establish rules. However, rules by definition regulate what is and what isn't allowed in a set of circumstances, many of which are usually bent or broken. Before any season starts, or when a new athlete joins my program, I believe it's important for the athlete and the parent to first understand the standards of the coach or the organization even before the philosophy or method of coaching is explained. Again, it all starts with laying down the standards from day one.

Standards of Excellence

I first learned about this from a basketball resource I was reading a few years back. It was about the NBA's Boston Celtics and their 'Standards of Excellence.' Later on I would read San Francisco 49ers' coach Bill Walsh's book, *The Score Takes Care of Itself,* and discovered that he also followed a similar philosophy.

Standards for the athlete or team are a foundation that are far superior to rules. Standards are guidelines to live by and hold each other accountable. I have often seen programs in sports organizations lose their way due to rules and standards either not being set, or not carried out by all those involved. It is the responsibility of the coach and the leaders within the group to make sure those standards are kept in place and adhered too.

I've discovered that all too often, coaches are quick to sit down and discuss tactics, goals, lesson structure, times of practices, and playing schedules, but the most important thing — standards — are either not addressed or simply brushed over. In coaching, we need to understand that we are in the behavior management business. When working with college or pro level athletes, egos are involved and some come with a sense of entitlement. Certain athletes feel they deserve special privileges, etc. This is something that needs to be addressed from the very beginning. Your best players and athletes need to be your best examples.

Again, as I've already mentioned, the standards and discipline of your program are going to be judged on the worst behavior you are willing to accept. If you allow poor attitudes, effort, and body language, then you are simply defining the standards you accept as a coach.

The standards and discipline of your program are going to be judged on the worst behaviour you are willing to accept.

Your standards are and must be 'controllables.' These are not standards that are unrealistic or unreasonable to ask. These are standards like bringing a great work ethic to practice, putting forth your best effort, having the right attitude, keeping disciplined, and staying committed. These are the things I ask of every athlete who works with me and the things for which he/she is held accountable.

In my training method, I have my athletes score themselves out of 5 on an 'A-F Standards Scorecard' after each practice, match or competition. It's a simple task that takes less than a minute to complete.

Standards Scorecard:

1. Attitude
2. Body Language
3. Commitment
4. Discipline

5. Effort

6. Fuel (hydration and food)

Having worked with many Olympians, world champions, and great athletes, I've learned that the one thing that stands out is their commitment to high standards for themselves and their team. They demand the best from themselves first, and then from those around them. They are relentless and will do anything to improve.

Observing great athletes like Jessica Innes, Nico Rosberg, Novak Djokovic, Serena Williams, Lebron James, Richie McCaw, Peyton Manning, Kobe Bryant, and many more, you realize how they put standards before anything else. They lead by example. Every day they wake up hungry to be better than the day before.

The great athletes are the ones who demand the best from themselves — not just sometimes, but all the time. That is why they have become great. What people don't realize is that when you reach the top or are very close to it, great athletic skills, game IQ, or technical skills are not enough to be the best. You need more than that. You need the standards and self-discipline of a champion.

The best athletes understand and believe in the 1%s, making the tiny marginal gains every day that add up to greater successes and results.

The best athletes also have higher standards in the 'uncomfortable' category. They have developed routines and habits that are of the highest level. They believe in the 1%s, making marginal gains every day and living up to their own personal standards. They practice attention to detail in their preparation, nutrition, equipment choices, sleep, and regeneration. They understand the fundamentals and importance of them. They understand that success is to be found in the repetition of purposeful, deliberate practice.

A good example comes from Eric Butorac. Eric is a top doubles tennis player and president of the ATP Player Council. He recently shared a great story about a practice with world no. 1 Novak Djokovic.

In Eric's words:

I had just lost a tight match in the third round of the 2015 US Open. I was in the back corner of the locker room. The TV in my area was tuned to the Grandstand court, so clearly someone had been following our match. I get a tap on the shoulder...it's Boris Becker. The conversation goes something like this:

BB: Eric, that was a great match...really high level.

Me: (Dejectedly): Yeah, thanks.

BB: No, really, I thought you guys played a great match.

Me: (Now officially out of the US Open): Yeah, it was OK.

BB: It really only came down to a couple of points.

Me: (Kind of tired of speaking about a match that he can't possibly care that much about): Most do.

BB: Listen, I know you just lost, but Novak really needs to practice with a lefty today because he plays Feliciano Lopez tomorrow. Do you mind?

Me: (It's about 100 degrees and humid, my hip is killing me, and I'm soaked from my two-hour match): Yeah. Sure.

BB: Great! Practice Court 1 in an hour!

I slowly walked out onto the row of empty practice courts and found a few thousand people anticipating our (or his) practice. It was one of those moments where going back on court was the last thing in the world I wanted to do, but now it is what I remember most about my US Open experience. I have practiced with a number of top players over the years. It's one of the perks of being left-handed, as those guys often need you to prep for a lefty opponent (thank you, Rafa). Most of my hits have been pretty relaxed, with Federer being the most casual of them all.

Novak was different. From the first ball, he was completely locked into the practice. Every ball he hit had a specific purpose. Every drill was designed to work on a specific situation that he would face against Lopez the next day. I was actually glad I'd had a match earlier in the day, because we only hit a few balls down the middle before things got intense. After only a few minutes, Becker ran over and asked if I could start chipping more backhands. Of course, I obliged. After one rally, he came running back and said, *"That's great. Now you are going to do only chip backhands...but don't just push them, really work Novak around the court."* I'm not sure how many of you have ever hit with Novak, but "working" him around the court with a chip backhand isn't exactly the easiest thing in the world to do. After 10 minutes of "working Novak around" with my chip backhand, I must have started to fade because he asked me to hit him some serves instead.

Me: Sure. Where would you like them? (In my hits with other top players, they like to get a rhythm off the slice serve first, then maybe a few kick serves, etc.)

Novak: Doesn't matter.

Me: You want me to hit some second serves to start, or start hitting first-serve speed?

Novak: Whatever.

Me: You don't want me to tell you where it's going at all?

Novak: Do you think Feliciano will tell me?

Novak went on to beat Feliciano and win the Open, his third Grand Slam of the year. Did my practice get him over the edge? Probably not. But it did give me a window into how and what the best player in the world does when he practices. I've always believed that I am organized and focused in practice, but he was on another level. I found that mindless hitting down the middle is not a great use of time. I discovered that fans would much prefer to watch me hit with Novak than to watch me play a doubles match! I knew that practicing your return was really important, but not more important than the way in which you practiced it. And I learned that I should work on my chip backhand, in case Novak ever called again.

The difference between the good and the great lies in their standards of excellence.

I spoke to multiple Grand Slam Champion Serena Williams' coach and a good friend of mine, Patrick Mourataglou at Wimbledon last year (2015) just before her 21st Grand Slam win. He mentioned how Serena not only demanded high standards within her team, but more from herself with every passing year. That's pretty impressive after almost 20 years on the professional tour.

Arguably one of the world's best ever soccer players who retired in 2015, USA's Amy Wambach said after their World Cup win in 2015, that success was found in the discipline and standards of each and every team member.

2011 and 2015 World Cup rugby winning captain, Richie McCaw of the All Blacks, always kept the highest of standards and demanded the same from his teammates. McCaw's style of leadership was one of example and of maintaining high levels in all areas. Bestselling author, speaker, and business consultant, James Kerr, talks about how the All Blacks operate in his best selling book, *Legacy*. He goes deep into the heart of the world's most successful sporting team to reveal 15 powerful and practical lessons for leadership and business. He asks questions such as: What are the secrets of sustained success? How do you achieve world-class standards, day after day, week after week, year after year? How do you handle pressure? How do you train to win at the highest level? If you haven't read his book, it's one I highly recommend.

Los Angeles Lakers star and owner of five NBA championship rings, Kobe Bryant, is another example of an athlete who leads by example. Kobe's work ethic and standards are of the highest level. It is well known that he would get to the gym to practice at 4:30 a.m. to work on certain elements of his game. Kobe was relentless in his preparation and demanded the same from those around him. I asked my friend Tim DiFrancesco, who is also the LA Lakers' head of strength and conditioning, about Kobe's standards and routines. This is what Tim had to say: *"You know, people ask me about his work ethic and if it's true that's he's the hardest working guy on the team, still at 36 years of age. Well, the answer to that is 'yes.' He is usually also the first to arrive at practice. Kobe is always asking for the next thing to do, be it extra stretching, strength work, sprints, whatever. His standards are so high that it's sometimes tough for some of the younger, newer guys to get to grips with it. He's an example of what every professional athlete should be!"*

When Coach Mike Krzyzewski, better known as Coach K, was choosing the squad of players for his 2008 Olympic team in Beijing, Kobe was one of his first picks due to his high standards, work ethic, and what Kobe could bring to the team (See Coach K's Gold standards below).

Higher standards are what give the athlete (and coach) the distinctive edge. They are what separate the good from the great.

Below I have listed my standards within the McCaw Method, as well as some of the coaches and organisations I have mentioned in this chapter. This should give you a great example and idea when it comes to setting out your standards.

McCaw Method Standards:

1. Time Management:

As I always like to explain to athletes, if you are late for practice or a meeting, it means that it's not important enough to you. The athlete is expected to arrive ahead of time, not on time. That means if practice starts at 8 a.m., then he/she is expected to be there no later than 7:40 a.m. You always have to take into account the time it takes to change clothes, tape up, prepare, chat to teammates, etc.

2. Body Language

This is a controllable. Not only does a poor body language show doubt and negativity, it also breaks down the mechanical side of the body, which leads to technical breakdowns. A positive body language is a powerful way of displaying confidence and energy. Showing poor body language results in handing off the positive traits to your opponents.

3. Communication (between coaches and fellow athletes)

We believe in communicating in a respectful manner, like letting the coach or our teammates finish speaking and not interrupting. We will also monitor our tone of voice. We prefer to criticize in private and compliment in public. We aim to respect others opinions, even if we might not always agree. We believe that becoming a great communicator involves becoming a great listener. When we talk we only say what we know, but when we listen we learn something new.

4. Dress code

Champions dress like champions. Champions look like champions. We take pride in our appearance. The goal is always to look neat, tidy and professional.

5. Preparation

We believe that great preparation is the difference between being ready and not being ready. We will be prepared with the necessary items, such as energy drinks, post practice shake, food, performance equipment, change of clothing, towel, first aid, etc.

6. No cell phones during practice

Cell phones are not permitted during practice time. We aim to limit distractions so we can focus and get the best from ourselves at all times.

7. Accountability

The athlete is responsible for knowing and carrying out his/her routines, such as warm-ups, cool downs, prehab, regeneration routines, etc. This is done at the highest of standards since these things are just as important as the 'big things.'

8. Bringing the right attitude and effort

We understand that we can all have tough times, but the athlete is expected to bring the right attitude and effort to every practice and competition. This contributes to a positive environment and the success of our program. We believe that if it's not 'your day' then try to make someone else's.

9. No excuses, only solutions

We don't have time for, or believe in excuses. We only look for solutions to the problems and challenges. We believe that excuses are for losers.

10. The right work ethic

We believe that hard work beats talent any day. There is no excuse why you cannot give your best effort. We thrive as a group and are proud that we won't be out-worked by anyone else. This is ingrained in our culture and mindset.

11. Helping others for the good of the team or fellow athletes

We might be opponents on match day (individual sports), but we will push and make each other better during practice time. Sometimes we need to help and assist coaches or fellow athletes and vice versa. Our attitude is about making each other better.

12. Commitment

We are committed to the task. We are committed to high standards of excellence. We are committed to getting 1% better every day. We are committed to improving ourselves, not just as athletes, but people.

13. Ability to accept feedback in a positive manner

We believe that to get better we need to be willing to hear the good and the bad. We believe that both negative and positive feedback will help us improve our game and ourselves. We will also receive this feedback without taking it personally, knowing it is beneficial to our growth and development.

14. Be process-driven, not result-driven

We believe that success is found in doing our best in the moment we are in. That involves staying in the process and trusting in the process. We believe that our best chance of succeeding and reaching our goals is taking care of the everyday things (routines and habits) to the best of our ability. We believe that when we take care of the process, the results will take care of themselves.

15. Always look to contribute to a positive environment.

We have no room for or acceptance of negative or bad behavior. We will contribute to building a positive and winning environment. This involves building each other up, magnifying each other's strengths, and supporting each other. We will look for every opportunity to grow our culture and environment.

16. This is a learning environment.

Mistakes are welcome. We desire to learn through our efforts and mistakes. Mistakes are an indication that we are trying. We aim to learn from our mistakes and we encourage feedback from our coaches to improve on these.

17. Always display good sportsmanship and respect.

We believe that the most important lessons we can get through sport are life lessons. We will conduct ourselves in the highest manner, behave accordingly, and show respect to all involved. We will show appreciation and gratitude to those who help and support us most (our parents, coaches, friends, etc.).

Bill Walsh's 10 Standards of Performance:

1. Ferocious and intelligently applied work ethic directed at continual improvement

2. Respect for everyone in the program and the work that he/she does

3. Commitment to learning

4. Demonstrate character and integrity

5. Honor the connection between details and improvement

6. Demonstrate loyalty

7. Be willing to go the extra mile for the organization

8. Put the team's welfare ahead of your own

9. Maintain an abnormally high level of concentration and focus

10. Make sacrifice and commitment the organization's trademark

Sir Clive Woodward's 15 Standards for the British Olympian Team in 2012:

PERFORMANCE

1) Hygiene.

2) 100% me. "The drug side of things, we want clean competition".

3) Being professional in everything we do. "Performance must come first. The performance of any individual athlete must come before any other individual responsibilities."

RESPONSIBILITY

4) Role Model. "That speaks for itself".

5) Time. "Timekeeping"

6) Accommodation. "Keeping your accommodation clean and tidy."

UNITY

7) Team. "That reads, 'naturally you will support your own sport but how great it would be if after you finish competing then you support all sports and all athletes until the final event is over'".

8) Ideas. "One of my favourite sayings is that there's no dumb ideas. If you can see anything that will improve the team or you think is wrong then as a team member you should bring that through to us."

9) Communication. "Making sure you understand who the team is and how you operate. We have a saying of 'no new faces'."

PRIDE

10) Kit. "It drove me nuts in Beijing because there were a couple of people who took great pride in walking around the village with a Nike T-shirt on. This is our sponsor [Adidas] and this is our team kit. All I'll say is that those athletes were nowhere near the podium and I'm not surprised because they didn't have the discipline."

11) Friends and family. "Making your friends and family part of all this so they understand how they need to operate because they can cause issues with social media as well".

12) Welcoming all other athletes from all other countries. "Taking real leadership in welcoming other athletes to the Games."

RESPECT

13) Social Media. "In many ways speaks for itself, it's handling Facebook and Tweeting in a responsible fashion. The definition reads: 'This will be a Games like no other with respect to social media and all the benefits and inherent risks that go with it. We will use social media responsibly at all times and ensure nobody is embarrassed by any actions taken through the use of social media'."

14) Language. "Very straightforward. In the confines of this room it might be acceptable to have colourful language but

when we're out in the public domain I don't expect any time would want to hear any bad language."

15) Noise. "It's common sense, it's noise in the Village. When you come back early in the morning or late in the evening it's not making noise, respecting not only our team but every other team. It's having your mobiles switched off so they're not going off in the middle of the night."

The NBA Boston Celtics 11 Standards of Excellence:

1. **PROFESSIONALISM:** We will commit to always conducting ourselves in a first class manner on and off the court every day of the year; this is a 24-hour/7 days a week commitment; we understand there is a difference between being in the pros and being a professional!

2. **NO PERSONAL AGENDAS:** We will commit to one agenda and one agenda only; that agenda will be doing whatever we are called on to do in order to help this team win a championship; our personal gains or situations will never come into play.

3. **PROFESSIONAL AND RESPECTFUL COMMUNICATION:** We will commit to listening to the "what" and not the "how," but will always be aware of how we are sending the message; let it be teammate to teammate and delivered with respect!

4. **THINK OF THE NOW ONLY:** We will commit to making sure everything we do is for the betterment of THIS TEAM-THIS YEAR; our personal situations will take a back seat to the team commitment!

5. **ONE WAY:** We will commit to teaching the system that we have; trusting the coaching and holding yourself accountable to do things the CELTIC WAY!

6. **EFFICIENT TEAM:** We will commit to executing our system with simplicity to ensure that we are productive and efficient in everything we do!

7. **TEAM OF EXECUTION:** We will commit to learning our system; understanding our system; and paying attention to the details of our system; understanding that when two equal teams meet, the team that executes better usually wins!

8. **NEVER HAVE A BAD PRACTICE:** We will commit to giving our best effort every day we hit the practice floor; at times understanding that we will have to pick our teammate up when needed!

9. **RESPONSIBILITY:** We commit to holding ourselves personally responsible and accountable for our actions; our efforts; and fulfilling the roles that we have been assigned; everyone will take responsibility for their role on our success.

10. **TRUST:** We will commit to this on a 24-hour/day basis; trusting each other in everything we do on and off the court; from talking on defense; to trusting that guys are getting their rest and taking care of their bodies; to trusting that everyone is representing each other in a first class manner at all times!

11. **NO EXCUSES:** We either get it done or we don't. Either way, we move on and make sure the next possession . . . the next quarter . . . the next game . . . is up to CELTIC STANDARD!

Coach K's Gold standards for the 2008 USA Olympic basketball team

1. No Excuses
- We have what it takes to win.

2. Great Defence
- This is the key to winning the gold.
- We do the dirty work.

3. Communication
- We look each other in the eye.
- We tell each other the truth.

4. Trust
- We believe in each other

5. Collective Responsibility
- We are committed to each other.
- We win together.

6. Care
- We have each other's back.
- We give aid to a teammate.

7. Respect
- We respect each other and our opponents.
- We're always on time.
- We're always prepared.

8. Intelligence
- We take good shots.
- We're aware of team fouls.
- We know the scouting report.

9. Poise
- We show no weaknesses.

10. Flexibility
- We can handle any situation.
- We don't complain.

11. Unselfishness
- We're connected.
- We make the extra pass.
- Our value is not measured by playing time.

12. Aggressiveness
- We play hard every possession.

13. Enthusiasm
- This is fun.

14. Performance
- We're hungry.
- We have no bad practices.

15. Pride
- We are the best team in the world and we represent the best country.

Eddie Jones Standards and Building a Sustainable Performance of Excellence

1. High work ethic always

2. Passion for detail

3. Get the right staff

4. Create a learning environment

5. Rules — make them very clear and understood

6. Meetings — no longer than 15 minutes

7. Communication — clear and concise

8. Evaluation — clear criteria, no gray areas

9. Books — read everything

10. Always look for a better way than the way you are doing it

Be the leader and coach your athletes need you to be.

What it boils down to is this: everyone needs to be on the same page. The standards of the whole organization from top to bottom need to be singing from the same hymn sheet. Standards, rules, and expectations need to be crystal clear from the beginning. The leadership in every situation needs to be willing to make corrections the moment they are needed.

Your athletes want to be disciplined. To some degree, they all want to work hard. Most of them simply don't know how. That is our job as coaches and leaders. It is our responsibility to give them the tools they need to be successful, not just in a sport, but in life. We need to show them how to be accountable and then hold them to it. It's our job as coaches to be the role model and leader they need.

Remember that great coaches set three kinds of standards.

1.Those for themselves,

2.Those for their organization

3.Those for the athletes they work with.

Coach Time:

1.What are you doing to improve the standards in your life every day?

2.What are your beliefs, core values, and principles?

3.What personal traits and characteristics do you admire in other successful coaches or people and would like to exemplify?

4.Would you follow your own example if you were an athlete?

5.What are the standards for your organization?

The degree of your success and results are related to the standards you have set.

CHAPTER 2

Method

"I believe every coach needs to have a method,
a system or philosophy."

- Allistair McCaw

There are three reasons why all coaches should have a method to the way they coach:

1. An identity.

2. It's what you believe in.

3. It's your training concepts and WHY.

1. An Identity

There is one common denominator I have discovered in observing, researching, and working alongside some of the best coaches in the world — they all have a philosophy, system, or method in the way that they coach and train their athletes and teams.

I believe that coaches should have an identity with the way they coach and operate. When it comes to a coaching method or philosophy, coaches should be able to describe **what** they believe in, **why** they believe in it, and **how** they do it.

A method and system can most easily be described as *a way of doing something.* In the athletic world of coaching, having a method is a systematic way of coaching and conducting your sessions. A method is also plan of action and an order in which you do things.

As a coach you are on a journey that will help you develop a method and create a dynamic philosophy that will continue to evolve throughout your career, allowing you to feel comfortable and confident in the way you make decisions and conduct your training sessions. Your method and philosophy will also comprise the values and standards you hold in highest regard and the ones you are comfortable sharing and teaching to the athletes you train and coach.

I have always found that **an effective and successful method is a simple one**. A method or system should also include your *WHYs, WHATs, HOWs* and *WHENs*. By this I mean you need to understand and be able to explain *why* you coach that way, *when* you use it, *how* you use it, and *what* you use it for.

Coaches need to know their WHYs, WHATs, HOWs and WHENs.

Simply explained, a method or system is the way you choose to train and work with your athletes. For example, it can include the strategies, exercises, drills, skills, and routines you set for your athletes and teams.

As we discussed in Chapter 1, the most successful coaching businesses, institutes, schools, academies, and organizations have high standards, a strong culture, and a positive environment. You will notice that they will also have a method or system of operation. A great example of this is the Bolshoi Academy.

The Bolshoi Academy

The Bolshoi Ballet School in Moscow, Russia is the most successful ballet academy in the world. It is also one of the toughest, if not the hardest schools to be accepted into. The school's head principal, Marina Leonova, explains that the system they have developed at the school is unique in its teachings and standards. For example, from the way they position a dancer's body parts, to the way they coordinate the movements, they operate within a system that involves producing the very best dancers in the world. They work from simple to complex and have built their reputation on a deep culture, high standards, sound teaching methods, and a highly disciplined work ethic.

Students attend classes from four to eight hours per day, always aiming at intense deep practices. The feedback style they receive can be harsh, direct and critical, but this is typical with Eastern European styles in teaching and coaching. As head principal, Leonova says: *"These are the best of the best, and we demand the best from these dancers every day."*

The Knicks

Phil Jackson has won more NBA rings than any other coach. Having coached the Chicago Bulls and LA Lakers, Jackson has always been about maintaining high standards and discipline from the teams he has coached. He is currently the president of the New York Knicks. I was listening to an interview with Jackson on ESPN recently where he talked about how important it is for everyone within the team and organization to understand and follow the system they have established there. In Jackson's words, *"We follow a set system within the Knicks that we all need to follow."*

The Sky Cycling Team

The Sky professional cycling team based in the UK competes in the famous Tour De France cycle race, a three-week grueling test of stamina and mental toughness. The Sky team is another great example of a system and method in motion. Their director of cycling, Dave Brailsford, is a leader who believes in what he calls the "marginal gains." The marginal gains apply to finding and implementing the "1%" each day — scrutinizing each fragment that encompasses the cyclists' and team's performance, and improving it by 1% — from an extra gram weight off the bike, to the quality of bed and pillows the rider sleeps on at night.

It's with those marginal gains and a winning method in action that Team Sky has seen two of its riders, Sir Bradley Wiggins and Chris Froome, claim victories in arguably one of the toughest endurance tests in sport.

You will notice that all great coaches have a method and system that works for them. You will often hear them talk about their philosophies and methods in interviews or press conferences. Coaches like former Dutch National Team and Manchester United's coach Louis Van Gaal, Doc Rivers of the LA Clippers, Chicago Cubs coach Joe Madden, the great golfing coach David Leadbetter and UCONN women's Basketball coach Geno Auriemma are prime examples.

Interview

Sometimes when I conduct a *McCaw Method Champion Coach* workshop, I will talk about the importance of having a method or system and I always like to explain it like this:

Lets say I am interviewing you all (attendee coaches) for the purpose of coaching a specific athlete. Let's say you all have the required qualities, years of experience, qualifications, and have worked with a few good athletes, here is my question to you: What is going to separate you from the group of coaches sitting in this room, and why should I choose you to train this athlete?

Firstly, here's the deal, you better be able to tell me what your coaching method, system, or philosophy is. Of course, all the attributes mentioned above are important regarding your experience, but I want to know what you stand for and how you coach. I want to know how you are going to make this athlete better and how you are going to achieve this. I want to know what your method and philosophy is. I especially want to know your why's and how's.

Many times I have posed this exact question to experienced coaches in a variety of sports, and many haven't been able to come up with a well rehearsed or solid answer. They stutter, "um" and "ah" when I ask them to explain to me their method of coaching. I tell them: *"You need an identity, because if you don't stand for something, you'll fall for anything!"*

You need an identity, something that sets you apart, makes you different.

Over the last 22 years, I have been working on developing my identity or method, and for more than half of that time, (the first 11 years), I wasn't even aware of it! However, in the second half of my coaching career, I have been experimenting and looking for ways to be a better coach, not only from exercises and drills, but also from people skills and a deeper understanding of the athlete developmental side.

Jurgen Klopp is the current manager/head coach of English Premier League club Liverpool. Klopp spent his entire 12-year playing career at Mainz 05 before going on to become their longest serving manager from 2001 to 2008, during which time they achieved promotion to the Bundesliga. In 2008, Klopp joined Borussia Dortmund, leading them in back-to-back Bundesliga wins in 2011 and 2012. Asked about his coaching method and philosophy, Klopp said, *"I believe your playing philosophy reflects your mentality, that reflects the club, that gives a direction to follow. You cannot play or operate without a method or philosophy in which all have bought into and understand."*

Developing an effective method or system takes time.

Not only should coaches have an identity in the specific elements they use to train athletes, whether in technical development, athletic skills development, strength training, power training, etc., but also in the way they bring forth their message to athletes and those they train. I've witnessed extremely smart and highly skilled coaches and trainers fail to connect with and communicate a message to their athletes in an effective and simple manner. Let's not forget that effective coaching is about Caring, Connecting, and Communicating.

Coaching is about Caring, Connecting and Communicating.

Let's put it this way. You are new in town and you are looking for a new doctor. You will probably ask a few friends or neighbors who they recommend. Of course, they will tell you that theirs is the best (otherwise they wouldn't be using that doctor). You then make a short list and research their backgrounds and experience. You would want to know how they work, what methods they use, and what they believe in. This is pretty much how it works in our industry.

To give you an idea, your method/system/philosophy should include:

1. Your style of coaching (matching your personality). Don't try and be someone you are not.

2. The methods in training, for example: speed training, strength training, skills (like developing a serve, a pitch, taking a free kick or a spike in volleyball), your approach to core training, exercises and drills you like to use, etc.

3. Your methods in building a positive environment and culture.

4. Your methods in developing high standards for the organization, your team, your athletes.

5. Your approach and method of developing an athlete or a player. For example, using the LTAD (Long Term Athlete Development).

6. The methods you use in the way you warm up, cool down, stretch, etc.

7. Your methods in recovery.

These are examples of the methods I'd want to know about you if I was interviewing you to work with an athlete, or team, plus how long you've been coaching, your qualifications, and your training experience.

What if I don't have a Method/System/Philosophy?

Here's the good news. If you have been coaching for a year or more, then you already have one! You just haven't written it down or documented it yet. Since you began coaching, you have already built up some kind of method and style without even knowing it. Every coach will have his/her 'go to' drills and exercises, or have a style of teaching a skill, for example, chunking (bit by bit) or a sequence. This indicates that you already have a system or method of working. However, you need to document it and know your *WHYs, WHATs, HOWs, and WHENs* (more on this to follow).

So how do you document a method or philosophy?

It's pretty simple. Start with a blank piece of paper. Sit down and write out the things you believe in and the practices you incorporate into training an athlete or team.

For example:

• I believe in performing a dynamic flexibility warm-up before any movement session.

• I believe that unilateral strength training is great for my athletes, as it helps eliminate imbalances in the body.

• I believe in drill X & Y for developing quickness.

• I believe in performing exercises N & M for improving the serve.

• I believe in rondos as a warm-up for my soccer players.

• I believe that each athlete needs between 7-9 hours of sleep per night.

• I believe that my athletes should consume 15 grams of protein within 20 minutes of completing a workout.

You can also set up a structure for conducting a training session. In my method I have athletes perform certain routines.

For example:

• Player performs a M.E.A.T. (Mobility, Elasticity, And myofascial Tissue) session before the first practice of the day (a 10-15 minute routine that involves soft tissue, flexibility, and mobility). In my method, we have the athletes first "prepare the meat" before we perform any kind of movement.

• Each warm-up for a racquet player (tennis, squash and badminton, etc.) is standard and consists of these four elements:

1. Agility (light warm-up of multi-directional movement)

2. Dynamic Flexibility And Mobility (FAM)

3. Hips (HB/HA)

4. Upper body band warm-up.

    • A warm-up for a ball player (football, rugby, lacrosse, soccer, etc.) is standard and consists of these four elements:

1. Agility (light warm-up of multi-directional movement)

2. Dynamic Flexibility & Mobility (FAM)

3. Hips (HB/HA)

4. Agility and footwork — more progressive in intensity

By having structure and routines in your method, you not only create an identity, but also a familiarity that the athlete understands and is accountable for.

In my method when starting with a new athlete or group, I spend the first few weeks teaching and integrating these routines. For example: The warm-ups, cool-downs, M.E.A.T routines, prehab routines, etc. for the athlete. When you spend time on the things that are often thought of as small details, and introduce and create the right routines and habits for the athlete, you have taken care of 50 percent of their chances for success. The rest comes down to hard work and their desire to be the best they can be. Again, the best athletes and teams are better prepared.

Spend time and be disciplined on the small details, but first have your fundamentals and 'big blocks' in place.

What are the advantages of having a method or system?

1. It gives you an identity to HOW you coach.

2. It helps with being prepared and well organized.

3. It prioritizes what is important and what isn't.

4. It provides your athletes with structure, clarity, and direction.

5. It keeps things simple.

A method helps keep things simple.

As I mentioned, when you are a life-long learner and are always looking for ways to improve yourself and your coaching skills, you will at times see something that just makes better sense. However, a big mistake a lot of coaches and trainers make is that they collect and accumulate a lot of 'stuff'. This results in complexity and information overload. Try not to keep adding things, rather subtract and look for ways to simplify your method. A simple method is a successful method.

I attended a Michael Boyle seminar in Dublin, Ireland, and one of the slides (that I 'borrowed' from him and sometimes use in my own presentations) states that, *if you still have the same system or method of training you had 10 years ago, you're either brilliant or your method stinks.*

The world is evolving and so are the coaching and training methods. As sports science and human performance information is advancing, we too need to stay on top of our game.

*Don't keep adding things,
rather subtract and look for
ways to simplify your method.
A simple method is
a successful method.*

2. It's what you believe in.

I believe that it's important as a coach to write down what you believe in. However, it's important as a coach to keep evolving and changing your mind. I don't mean you are changing your mind because you just feel like it, or feel you have to. Nor does it imply that you are indecisive or unsure. It simply means that as a lifelong learner, you are finding ways to do it better and smarter.

Listen, look, learn, ask and write everything down.

The late and great coach John Wooden, was known to sit and listen to other coaches at talks or workshops and then furiously take down notes. It's incredible that a coach of this magnitude was still willing to listen and learn from others who didn't have half the experience or accolades he had. He was always looking for ways to improve his coaching skills and players, and was willing to learn from just about anyone! Talk about a humble man. It still amazes me to see people who attend seminars or talks by other coaches and not bother to take notes. It's impossible to remember everything, so try to get into the habit of writing things down.

You might wonder what makes Jose Mourinho, one of football's most controversial and successful coaches, so outstanding. Sir Bobby Robson, who hired Jose as a young assistant coach at Barcelona FC, said the young coach from Portugal listened intensely, watched everything, asked questions, and wrote everything down. Mourinho was compiling his own philosophy or method for coaching, which would help him eventually go on to capture the Italian, English, Portuguese and Spanish championship titles.

Stand for something or you will fall for anything.

Your method or philosophy of coaching is a collection and accumulation of all your past experiences: knowledge, people you've met, mentors, books you've read, study courses, things you've watched, listened to, your own playing or competing experiences, personal beliefs, values, principles, and time spent actually coaching. No one has the perfect strategy or method, not even the great coaches. They are always trying to find new ways to get better, because they understand that the better they become as a coach, the better they can make their athletes.

What matters is that you have a method and you believe in it. Again, it's not something that should be set in stone. When you are a life learner and a coach with a passion to improve, you will at times change your perceptions and rework some things. Not everyone is going to agree with your way of coaching, but they will respect the fact that you have faith in what you're doing.

2013 Wimbledon Tennis Champion, Marion Bartoli, is a player I had tracked since she was 16. She played against a few athletes I worked with, namely Nathalie Dechy, Dinara Safina (former world no. 1), Svetlana Kuznetsova (former world no. 2 and 2-time Grand Slam Champion) and a few more. Marion was coached by her father, Walter. His nickname on the tour was '*The Scientist*' due to his eccentric and diverse ways of coaching. Walter was always designing and inventing new gadgets to help train Marion. Sometimes you would see her on the court with these cables, harnesses, and other objects which stirred up a good amount of interest at the practice courts and gyms. She had a very different technique than the other players. In fact, it's not a technique you would see other coaches emulating. Personally, I always admired Walter. He wasn't afraid of taking risks and trying something new. He didn't care what others thought.

The lesson we can all learn from this is: Walter and Marion believed in their system despite the constant teasing and jibes. The result? - A system and philosophy that produced a Wimbledon champion.

Better to have a mediocre method or system and believe in it, than to have a world-class system, but continually be doubting it.

Another great coach I was fortunate to spend some time with was Shaun Moxham, coach of former two-time world squash champion, and world no. 1, David Palmer. Shaun was always busy writing things down. He documented every athlete, every lesson, and had a method that produced many great players. I would sometimes see Shaun on the court alone, rehearsing some of his lessons and practicing the drills he would be taking his players through that day. In fact, David Palmer now runs a successful academy out of Orlando Florida, and brings some of his players to train with me from time to time. David is now an incredible coach himself.

A commonality of all of the great coaches I've worked with (World Cup winning rugby, cricket, and hockey teams, PGA and LPGA Golf Champions, Olympic medalists, Squash world champions, Grand Slam winners) is that they all had a documented method and style of coaching. These coaches over the years, through trial and error, victory and defeat, developed their way of coaching and leading their athletes and teams.

What matters is that you have a method and you believe in it.

Coach Tip: *Spend time observing successful coaches. See how they do things and what methods and systems they follow. Read and research good coaches and learn from them.*

Better to have a mediocre method or system and believe in it, than to have a world-class one, but continually be doubting it.

3. Your training concepts

The WHYs, WHATs, HOWs, and WHENs

To have an effective and successful method or system you need to know:

- WHY you do/use/endorse it?
- WHAT you use it for?
- HOW you use it?
- WHEN you use it?

The *WHYs*

Anyone who has read Simon Sinek's book, '*Start with Why*', will already know what I'm talking about when I say you need to start with *WHY*. Your *WHY* is your deeper purpose and reason as to why you do something. World-class athletes are a pretty sharp and switched on group of people. They want to know *WHY*. **When you are working with this level of athlete, you need to know your whys and be convincing about them.** For example, they want to know why they are doing a certain exercise, or why they are not doing something they did last week in their program, etc.

A mistake I see all too often is coaches and trainers taking information from the Internet or YouTube and having their athletes mimic it, without having a clue as to why they are doing it. They seem to think that if it's good enough for Lebron, Ashour, Ronaldo, Phelps, or Djokovic, then it must be good for their player. This, unfortunately, is not a strong enough *WHY*. In fact, I have seen 10-year-old kids forced through the same drills and exercises as these above-mentioned athletes. Some parents and coaches think that these drills and exercises will increase their kids' chances of becoming champion athletes, when in fact the complete opposite usually happens – Injury, burn-out and overload.

A coach who understands his WHYs will also be ahead of a coach who only understands his HOWs.

You need to have a reason *WHY* you do things the way you do. Just like every lesson you plan must have goals and a purpose, so too must the exercises and drills you choose. It's not about having the best drills or exercises, it's about having the right ones for your athlete or team. It's about knowing and understanding why you are prescribing certain things to your athletes. Elite level athletes want to know *WHY.* So as a coach, you need to have your answers and explanations lined up and ready to deliver.

Everything you do must have a purpose and a WHY.

The *WHATs*

The *WHATs* have more to do with the things you use within your method. When implying the *WHAT,* we need to know what the best things are for that athlete at the right time. The *WHATs* cover the exercises and drills you use when training your athletes. For example, *WHAT* exercises and drills you use to develop an athlete's speed or strength; *WHAT* method you use to improve a player's pitch or serve; *WHAT* tools you use to develop an athlete's core power, etc.

In my method we use the half foam rollers for single leg strength, stability, and balance training. We will always use the McCaw Method stretch straps for improving range of motion and hip mobility after each training session. These are things that give my program and method some identity.

The *WHATs* can include the elements and methods you believe in, for example, having your athletes perform plyos, single leg work on a half foam roller, myofascial release work, working on a physio ball, BOSU, etc.

The *HOWs*

The *HOWs* are the easiest part. However, it's finding the right *HOWs* that matter most. Everywhere we look there are so many platforms to obtain exercises and drills. Every day thousands of videos are uploaded and posted on multi-media sites, like YouTube, Instagram, Twitter, Facebook, etc. The challenge is sifting out the quality from the rubbish. You see, today we are inundated with information. But the challenge is to find who and what is authentic and what isn't.

Great coaches know the *HOWs* better than the others. For example, they know *HOW* to match the right exercises or drills at the right time for the right athlete. Young coaches need to understand that this is where experience and the years of trial and error come to fruition. **Great coaching involves great timing**. Today, we have numerous gurus and experts out there, but when we try to find out who they have trained, the list comes up blank. I've always said that some of the best coaches in the world are not the ones you see on TV or at the Pro Bowl, they are coaches you and I will probably never hear of, in far away places we will never visit.

It's not about having the best drills or exercises, it's about having the RIGHT ones for your athletes at that particular time.

Great coaches are also great demonstrators. They know their *HOWs* and it's been proven that people best learn by using all three forms of auditory, visual and kinesthetic methods (I will discuss this in more details later in the book).

Like a school teacher who prepares her lessons, I personally spend about an hour a week going through exercises or drills before I actually have my athletes do them, in order to correct and perform them to the best of my ability. I will sometimes either perform the exercise or movement in front of a mirror, or record it so I can view it. **Demonstrating the *HOW* is a big part of my job**. If I am showing a poor example in demonstrating it to my athletes or groups, it doesn't give credit to my coaching methods or standards.

Demonstrating the HOW is a big part of a coach's job.

The *HOWs* are also about the way you do things within your business or method. This is something that takes time to develop and integrate. As I mentioned, when athletes start training with me, I take the first few weeks to spend time on and integrate routines and structures into their daily lives. I show them how to do it and explain why. Again, explaining the *why* and the *how* is important to the athlete.

Showing your *HOWs* is a huge reflection on the quality of your program or method. You might be the Albert Einstein of coaching, but if your demonstrations are poor, you won't have a positive impact on your athletes or those you are teaching.

How you do things is also closely related to the standards you keep.

Coaches don't rush the *HOWs*. Be sure to take your athlete through each contributing factor within your method or system. Spend time on the 'small things' that are actually huge, in my opinion, like *HOW* your athletes warm up, *HOW* they prepare, *HOW* they cool down, *HOW* they stretch, etc.

I have always been able to assess the standards and how effective a coach is by simply observing his or her player's warm-up. It's a small observation that gives me so much information, even before seeing how they perform.

The best athletes have been coached to do the small things incredibly well. Why? Because they understand that it all matters. It also shows their focus and attention to detail. Sloppy warm-ups, cutting corners, etc., show the quality of a program and a reflection of the standards of the coach.

I have always been able to see the standards and how close to the small details a coach is, just by observing his or her player's warm-up.

Coach Wooden was famous for guiding his players through some of the basics, like telling them how to put on their socks properly to avoid blisters. As we know, blisters can prevent an athlete from playing or practicing. He would also teach them how to tie their shoelaces with a double knot so there would be no possibility of wasting time during competition. Otherwise, a shoelace became untied, or worse, a player unnecessarily tripped and fell.

Personally, I always take pride in seeing my athletes take these meticulous steps and stay focused. This shows quality and depth in my method and how I do things.

Last but not least, if you don't know how, then ask and learn how. Great coaches are not afraid to ask for help when they need it.

The thing is, when you're aiming for excellence,
IT ALL MATTERS.

Great coaches know their WHYs.

The *WHENs*

The *WHENs* are a big one. The *WHENs* are something that you get better at the longer you are in the game of coaching. The *WHEN* is all about gaining the knowledge and then the experience — knowing *WHEN* to do something or use something.

I will never forget a huge mistake I made about 12 years ago. I was warming up an elite badminton player who had just started with me that day (I know, not ideal). It was just before a tournament. I took her through my (mistake nr.1: "*my*"), usual warm-up routine of the agility, dynamic flexibility, hips and upper body resistance tube routines. Fast forward to the match. After a disastrous start and display, my player looks over at me after the first game and says she's cramping and can hardly move! Now I'm thinking that this is an elite high-level badminton player in a tough sport and she's struggling after just one game! What on earth is going on? Well, needless to say, she lost that match and I discovered that the nature of the warm-up and the dynamic flexibility exercises I put her through were obviously too advanced and were movements that she was not accustomed to. This was a good lesson for me and an example of *WHEN* to start or introduce exercises, or even a 'basic' warm-up routine for a new athlete. **The *WHENs* are usually our best teachers.** Knowing *WHEN* to introduce new exercises or drills, or *WHEN* to change, add, or subtract from an athlete's program, is the sign of a good coach. Another example is not performing a leg workout or plyo routine a day or two before competing. These kinds of decisions in your planning and timing are huge when it comes to getting the respect from those you train, as well as their belief in your coaching skills. We get better at this with experience.

The WHENs are usually our best teachers. Knowing WHEN to say something, WHEN to introduce new exercises or drills, or WHEN to change, add, or subtract from an athlete's program.

And regarding building confidence in my athletes, the final 2 or 3 days leading up to a tournament, competition, or race are used for building and polishing their confidence. I focus on their strengths and let the athletes feel like they are taking more of the lead. I don't push drills or exercise on my athletes just before a competition; in fact I let them choose. Why? - Because they will usually choose the things that give them the most confidence, and that's what matters most!

The McCaw Method

Within my method I have four pillars. It is within these four pillars that I build and design an athletes or team's program. Each pillar incorporates the elements and routines that I follow as a coach. These also include the routines, exercises, drills, mindset, and motivation strategies that I implement when training an athlete or team.

The foundation of these four pillars is supported by 3 things:

1. STANDARDS

2. FUNDAMENTALS

3. PREPARATION

The Four pillars of the McCaw Method:

1. **MOVEMENT:** This covers all the elements of the athletes' movement skills. For example, their speed skills, agility skills, sport-specific movement patterns, etc..

2. **MINDSET:** This covers the mental preparation and thought process of the athletes during practice and competition time.

3. **MUSCLE:** This covers their strength and power development. For example, their plyometric routines, core power, unilateral strength, etc.

4. **MOTIVATION:** This covers what I call the 'fire in the belly.' It's important for me as a coach to know what motivates my athletes.

An example of some of the routines for athletes within my method:

1. The 4 x 4 warm-up routine before all practices and training sessions

2. The M.E.A.T. routine: Flexibility, Mobility And Tissue (myofascial routine) every 12 hours

3. HB/HA: Hips Before and Hips After every practice (strength before, mobility after)

4. Incorporating an agility game for 5-10 minutes before practice

5. B.U.F.: Balance Under Fatigue: I will have my athletes perform some balance and stability exercises after each practice for maybe 2-4 minutes

6. Stretch Strap routine after each practice session.

I hope this chapter better explains why every coach needs to have a system or method. Remember, not to become too rigid in your method, nothing should be cast in stone. As you keep evolving and learning, you will tweak and change things from time to time.

Coach Time:

1. Why do you feel you need a method or system in your coaching?

2. Do you already have a method or philosophy in place?

3. Have you documented your method and philosophy?

4. Would you be able to tell me today what your method is all about?

5. Do you know and understand your WHYs, WHATs, HOWs and WHENs?

CHAPTER 3

Adapt

"The Only Thing that is Constant is Change"

- Heraclitus

In this chapter I have divided it into 3 areas:

1. Change is constant.

2. Understanding the Generation You are Working with.

3. Understanding the Athletes Different Learning style.

I. Change is Constant

If there's one thing I've learned through my years of being a performance coach and working in the athlete enhancement field, it's the fact that change happens and learning never stops. At some point change will occur. Change is good, and when accepted, it typically is followed by personal or professional growth.

Your best bet is to take change as a positive thing, do not fear it. **Change will come, and how you embrace and receive it will determine how far you go.** As I mention in this chapter, some changes are controllable and some are not. Everyone has an opportunity to become great, but you need to create the opportunities and not be afraid of change.

In the previous chapter, we spoke about being a life-long learner and how you should have a mindset to get better than you were the day before. When it comes to coaching, as a life-long learner, the development of your system or method is never complete. Remember that the life-long learner changes his or her mind from time to time due to discovering smarter or better ways to proceed.

Something that occurs all too often with coaches who have been in the game for a while, is that they get too comfortable. They seem to reach a certain level of comfort because of age, success, or job security. For some, it can be harder to accept change. Often when coaches feel like they've 'got it,' they're inviting trouble.

When coaches feel they've 'got it,' they're in trouble. Always stay curious and uncomfortable.

Personally, I know that if I don't keep track of things that are going on in the industry, even just for a month, I feel I've missed something. One habit I have is checking Twitter while waiting for someone or standing in a supermarket line. This has been a fantastic tool for keeping up-to-date with the new information in our industry, as well as staying connected with other coaches. If you aren't on these social media platforms, I highly recommend you get connected to keep up-to-date with the happenings in the industry.

Another great tip is to start your own Facebook page for your business, if you don't already have one. Creating a page that provides information about you and your business is a great advertising tool. Also, try to include some interesting bits of information for your followers; for example, tips on training, coaching, and self-improvement.

Just this past December I met a football coach at a seminar where I was giving a presentation. His name was Tom, and he was probably around the age of 60. After my presentation he approached me to chat, and I asked him if he was on Twitter or Facebook, and how he kept up-to-date with the industry and the developments in the sports performance field. His reply was quite surprising to me. He said, *"I don't do any of those things. Those are for the younger people. Even email was a bit of a challenge for me to get into!"* Tom went on to tell me that the fundamentals don't change, to which I wholeheartedly agreed, but he didn't see a reason why he needed to know what was new in the coaching world. With this kind of attitude in a fast changing environment, people like Tom are going to struggle to stay in the game. This is an example of not being willing to change and adapt.

Any opportunity to learn is an opportunity to learn and move forward.

You might remember Coach Boyle's quote from chapter 2, *"If you are still running the same program that you where 10 years ago, you are either a genius or your program stinks!"* This statement implies that if you are not willing to learn, change, and adapt, you are going to be in trouble . . . or hey, you're just a straight out genius!

A performance coach I admired many years ago is another example of how important change is. Without mentioning any names, he was one of the 'main guys' in Athlete Development. However, one thing he failed to do was change and adapt. He stuck to his old ways of training and coaching and didn't really make an exerted effort to advance his knowledge and expertise in the business. Many top athletes started to leave once they found his training was still 1970's style. Even though burpees and jumping jacks might get you 'fit,' they didn't make you a better athlete in the sport you were playing. Before you jump on my back for insinuating that the training was bad back then, what I am really saying is that with sports science and the advancement of our industry, there are now better and safer ways to develop and enhance an athlete's performance.

Today I still enroll in fitness and sports performance summits and conferences. Each year I try to enroll in three to four courses and schedule two of those from different sports that I have never been involved in. I believe that a great coach learns from anything and everyone. **I have probably been to hundreds of seminars and workshops, and I have always had the mindset that if I can learn just one new thing, it's been worthwhile.** Even the ineffective conferences or presentations I have been to have always taught me something. Remember that learning is not only about what to do, but also what not to do. I believe that any opportunity to learn is an opportunity to grow and move forwards.

Learning from Other Coaches

It's important to watch other coaches in the industry and learn. It's important to learn not only from your own mistakes, but from others' mistakes. This certainly speeds up your learning process.

It's important to watch other coaches in the industry and learn.

Learn from everyone (and I mean *everyone*), not only the experienced and well-known coaches, but also from the new ones fresh from their certification classes and ready to take on the world.

One of the qualities of a great coach is their flexibility to change, while remaining true to his/her core values, standards, and principles. Even though the sport you are coaching doesn't change, the athletes do. I know from experience in dealing with different age groups, that to connect with these different generations, you need to be up-to-date with their music choices, interests, and especially the way in which they communicate. This is another key point for successful coaching today. You need to adapt to the individual.

Even though the sport you are coaching doesn't change, the athletes do.

As coaches we need to realize that we are working with separate and unique individuals, even if their sport is the same. This is where the quality of a coach's understanding and ability to connect and communicate comes in. The more athletes you work with over time, the more experience you gain in understanding and knowing how to deal with certain situations. As a coach you need to be open to change and accept differences of opinion. Remember that an opinion is simply another person or party's view, and not a fact. Believe me, I've seen some small differences of opinion, like disagreeing about a drill or exercise, result in the break-up of working relationships and partnerships. Worse, they have ruined environments. In my own experience, I have learned that what used to bother me 10 years ago, now no longer does, as I have been through those experiences and am now better equipped to handle them.

The 'great coach' is a coach who understands the different generations, and knows how to connect with them.

There's no school like the old school, but sometimes the old school ways just have to go. I am referring to the ways in which we discipline and communicate with our athletes today. I often hear coaches say things like, *"Back in my day we wouldn't tolerate that behavior,"* or, *"This generation has no respect."*

The old 'my way or the highway' approach just won't work today. We need to understand that we are dealing with a new generation that communicates, socializes, and interacts differently than the generations that came before. However, they are a generation that seeks discipline and leadership, but in a different way to how we received it growing up. I will discuss this more in detail further in this chapter.

With a 'my way or the highway' style of coaching, you won't retain many clients or athletes.

We work in an amazing and interesting industry. Sometimes we have to work with athletes or clients that we maybe don't particularly like or don't choose to spend time with. There is a very small percentage of coaches who have the luxury of choosing to work with whomever they want, but for the rest of us, working with academies, teams, colleges, clubs, and sports groups, we don't necessarily get to choose our athletes.

This is another area where you need to be able to adjust and adapt well. The key here is to see the best in others, not always easy, I know. Unfortunately, many coaches don't see the potential in athletes, they just see what they have at that moment. I can tell you that there is no better challenge than to work with that kid who no one else wants to train. For example, the kid who has the worst balance, coordination, and athletic skills — this is where great opportunity lies — in places where others don't want to go. This is where you grab your chances!

Go to where others aren't willing to go. Do what others aren't willing to do.

That is where opportunity and success lie.

See the potential in others and consistently point out their strengths. Our job as coaches is to magnify others' strengths and build on them. These athletes have already had every coach tell them what they can't do. **Great coaches show their athletes what they CAN do.**

Working as a professional, it's also important to keep work separate from your personal life. Becoming too friendly can result in a loss of respect from the athlete. Remember that there is a difference between being friends and being friendly. As a coach, it's better to be respected than liked. However, being liked is a definite plus for making more of a connection!

Remember, it's better to be respected than to be liked as a coach.

Four Areas Where Great Coaches Adapt

1. Great coaches adapt to the athlete better.

Even though the sport may be the same, no athlete is the same. Every athlete comes with a different package. These packages can include cultural backgrounds, family type, spiritual beliefs, upbringing, coaching techniques, values, mindset, etc. This is why it's important to first understand the athlete and how he/she has been raised. We need to realize that not everyone is raised with the same values, principles, standards, and beliefs as ourselves. We need to respect that.

Great coaches are able to learn and understand their athletes better, not just from an athletic or game point of view, but from all the areas I have mentioned above. Adapting to the athlete and his/her way of thinking, learning, and communicating is the key to successful coaching. The generation you are teaching also requires that you get to know them better. There are numerous books to help coaches learn this concept. One example is *Generation iY* by Tim Elmore. In the end, it's all about making the effort to really get to know the athletes you are coaching, and learning the way they operate and think.

Great coaches see the best in others. They see what can be, and not what is. When you have this mindset and vision, things dramatically change.

I have found that my most demanding and difficult athletes have given me my best learning experiences. They have made me a better coach. When I refer to a 'demanding athlete,' I am talking about an individual who wants to improve and keeps asking *WHY*. **You will find that most of the best athletes are not easy to work with, and that is why a great coach with good interpersonal skills always rises to the top.**

Working with eight-time world champion and former world no. 1 in squash, Nicol David, I discovered that she was unique in how she performed on and off the court. When Nicol stepped onto the court, she was a hard-as-nails opponent. However, off the court, you wouldn't find a more gentle natured and laid back person.

At the same time, I was working with former world number 1 in tennis, Dinara Safina, whose personality was more intense, on and off the court. Nicol could switch off when away from the court, but Dinara would spend time in deep thought about her game and how she could get better. Both are hard working and fantastic girls on and off the court, but unique in so many ways. I had to adapt and adjust every time I worked with them. I had to adapt to their personalities and approach each in a different way. Ultimately, it has made me a better coach.

Delaney Collins, a three-time world champion ice hockey player who I worked with for a short period back in 2010, said it best during one of our training sessions. She said, *"Macca, dial into me, man!"* — meaning connect, listen, and understand me! Again, proof that as coaches we are always learning and need to be reminded to 'dial' into our charges to become better coaches. Because ultimately, a great coach's main goal should be to adapt and connect with the goal of making the athlete better. Adapting to athletes is also about listening to them more intensely and letting them express their feelings. I have always believed that the most powerful question you can ask an athlete is *"What do you think?"*. Delaney made me a better coach, as she taught me to listen and tune in better.

The best coaches are 80 percent listeners and 20 percent talkers. **When you talk, you are already saying something you know, but when you listen, you learn.**

I have always believed that the most powerful question you can ask an athlete is: "What do you think?"

One of the nicest and easiest athletes I've ever worked with in my whole career was tennis professional Xavier Malisse. I got to work with Xavier later in his career and it taught me a lot about the importance of adapting and listening to the athlete. The 'X man,' as he's known, had already reached high levels in his career, beating players like Roger Federer and Rafael Nadal, as well reaching the semi-finals in Wimbledon. Xavier has a great personality, is laid back, and enjoys having fun. I had to adapt to his ways, knowing that too much seriousness and a 'hard work' only mentality would not suffice. At the age of 32, Xavier knew what he needed to get back into the top 40 in the world, so even with all my experience in training athletes, it was important that I listened to him about what he felt he needed and how much.

Rather than logging loads of hours, together we devised a training program that would get him back in the game. After almost 16 years on the tour, it was important to keep him motivated and make the work/coaching as fun as possible. At that stage in his career, he was not excited about doing footwork or agility drills. Too much 'specific' training would not work. So, knowing that he loved to play games and different sports, we planned a program that included a variety of fun and games. For example, to get him to do footwork, I would have him combine a ladder drill, then shoot a basketball, sometimes multiple reps against a clock. It kept it fun and challenging. I would say that the ratio of tennis training time to physical was 20/80 when we worked together. I adapted to what he needed, and not what was on my agenda. If I had come into this working relationship with a *'my way or the highway'* approach, this would not have worked. This is one lesson we can learn as coaches, especially while working with more experienced athletes – listen more. I believe that this is one of the main differences between working with younger athlete and the more experienced. As coaches, we need to listen to them more intensely as in most cases, they know what they need to succeed, they just need us for the motivation and to provide structure.

Listen intensely to the more experienced athletes; they know themselves better.

2. Great coaches adapt to different situations better.

When we are talking about 'situations,' we could also mean *change* or *the unexpected.* In athlete performance and sport, we know we are in an industry where things are constantly changing. Some are 'controllables' and some aren't. This is where it starts for the coach: separating the things you can control and the things you can't. Great coaches are able to do this extremely well. Through many experiences, coaches have taught themselves how to handle stress and keep a cool head at the same time.

Great coaches invest in their mindset. They have a great interest in improving themselves in this area and love to read and research how best to handle pressure situations and adapt to change. They have developed clear thinking strategies and understand that their ability to handle different situations is what gives their athletes and teams confidence in them.

For every two books I order, I make sure that at least one is on the subject of personal development. As a coach, I believe that coaching is 20 percent of the Xs & Os, and 80 percent the interpersonal skills in dealing with people. **I find that many coaches spend far too much time trying to build their exercise and drill library thinking that this is the best way to improve their athletes, when in fact, the best way to improve their athletes is to first improve themselves — as a person and as a coach.**

"A great coach is like a chameleon. They adapt to the environment they are in and don't feel they need to be making a noise all the time."

- Allistair McCaw

Improvement starts with "I."

Great coaches can handle change and adapt quicker, no matter what is thrown at them. Whether their best player gets injured just before a big match, or there is a change in the team's opponents or venue, great coaches are able to switch to a 'solution' mindset and move forward quickly. They have a way of seeing the positive in a bad situation.

Great coaches are solution seekers and problem solvers. They love a good challenge because it gives them an opportunity to build trust and connection with their athletes. In a way, they love to show their metal under pressure. They know that their athletes are watching them the whole time, especially when an unexpected change or pressure situation occurs. This provides coaches an ideal opportunity to show their resilience and control.

In the end, it's all about being prepared, being able to find solutions, and expecting the unexpected. The more experiences you encounter, the more you learn how to deal with them. When you are able to do this, your coaching skills and reputation reach a higher level.

The best way to improve others is by first improving yourself.

3. Great coaches adapt to the different environments better.

Chameleons are amazing creatures. They can adapt to any environment and blend in. They blend in so well that they become almost invisible. They don't make much noise or feel they need to either. I love using the chameleon example when I describe what a coach should be like. Great coaches adapt very much like a chameleon to the environment they are in.

A lesson I've learned while working with athletes in different countries is that it's important to learn and understand their culture and environment, for example, where they have come from and 'how things work' there. The manner in which things are done in places like China, Russia, Serbia, and Romania are way different than how they are done in the U.S. or U.K. From their teaching methods and the way they develop an athlete, to the way they communicate or interact, as coaches, we need to embrace, learn, and better understand them. Attempting to change their cultural habits will most likely result in a return ticket home.

When comparing my work with athletes who have been brought up in an Eastern European country with athletes from the United States, I have found that feedback and communication are delivered very differently. For example, in Eastern European countries, the feedback can be more direct and ruthless to the athlete. In my experience working with world class athletes and their coaches from these countries, they have a 'good is not good enough' attitude. More time is spent criticizing the athletes rather than complimenting them. On the other hand, here in the United States we prefer to compliment more, sometimes too often, shouting "good job" every 15 seconds.

A few years ago whilst working in Moscow, Russia with a world top five female tennis player, I had a memorable experience. Her mother, who also happened to be her coach since age five, was highly respected and had worked with many great players, including several Grand Slam champions in the women's and men's games. It was the first day of practice in the Spartak Moscow Club, just after arriving from playing a tournament in Luxembourg. About five minutes into the practice, I complimented the player for her great effort on reaching a ball, when suddenly her mother shouted and demanded that play be halted. As she approached me, I could see by her body language and demeanor that she was not happy. She said in a thick and heavy Russian accent, *"Why do you compliment her on that? That is something she SHOULD be doing every time, and it's something that doesn't need to be complimented."* At first I was shocked and I had to stand back and digest what she had just said. This was an important lesson for me, to accept the way they work in her country. In these cultures and environments you have to really earn a "well done." You have to do something extraordinary to warrant a compliment. (Also see "False Feedback Fails" article at the end of this chapter).

Personally, my coaching style is to call it as I see it in a truthful manner. I believe that athletes need a combination of positive feedback and information (not criticism) to develop. However, one thing I will always compliment is a great effort, because a great stroke or shot can be a one-time lucky moment, but an effort or work ethic is a purposeful action. The athlete needs to be rewarded for the right things, not only for the results.

Rewarding the 'right things' would include:

- Attitude
- Work ethic
- Body language
- Effort
- Communication
- Teamwork
- Discipline
- Preparation

I will always compliment and place great effort &
work ethic over results.

My main point here is that as a coach, I need to adapt, and not try and change the environment I am working in. I need to understand the commonalities and differences and come up with the best solution for all involved, not just my own needs. I have been privileged and blessed to have worked with many athletes and their teams from all different parts of the globe, and I believe the key to sustaining these relationships and working collaborations has been due to understanding and adapting to their culture and environments better.

Having worked in a diverse range of sports, such as tennis, golf, and squash — mostly individual disciplines, as well as rugby — like NFL Football, a hard hitting team sport, one thing that resonates is that the coaches' personalities and the way they approach their players differ vastly. For example, in rugby, a raised voice and more 'aggressive' approach is sometimes necessary, but in a sport like tennis or golf, that approach can have a completely opposite effect.

During my years living in South Africa, I worked with former South African Rugby Vice Captain James Dalton. James was a fantastic leader, but there were times when he would let his fiery temper get the best of him. I cherished my one-on-one time with James during our training sessions in a Sandton gym in Johannesburg. I learned so much from him about the dynamics of adapting, connecting, leadership, and teamwork.

During that time I also had the privilege of working with the Falcons Super 14 team and the Northern Bulls ladies team. Both were great experiences, and although the sport was the same, each player demonstrated individualism. I had to adjust and adapt my coaching methods to their unique personalities.

To know what qualities make a great coach, we need to understand what great coaching is. Arguably, the job of any coach is to help his athletes realize their potential. Some would claim that training a top 10 player in the world is the sign of great coaching. However, if that player had the potential to be number 1, he/she may need an even better coach. Thing is, I might have got 'lucky' getting that player, so the fact that I maybe coach a top player doesn't make me a great coach.

Back in 2001, I had a contract to work in Sicily. My job description entailed managing and coaching a professional cycling team. The team included riders from various countries, such as Germany, South Africa, England, Italy, and France. Anyone who understands the Latin/Italian culture and their siestas (daytime naps) will know that nothing happens in those parts of the world between two and five p.m. When I first began working there, I wanted to plan training rides or gym sessions when traffic was less busy, but found it incredibly difficult and frustrating to get a gym or support team because everyone was sleeping! I had to conform to their way of living and adapt to the sleep and work patterns of the island.

A closer-to-home example of adaptation is learning to adapt to different colleges or universities in the United States when I am consulting. One of the first things I do is research their values and mission statement to understand their culture and environment. I need to conform because I am the one who is the 'outsider.'

These things are important in building and sustaining a successful and happy relationship. One particular university I consult with is Southern Methodist University (SMU) in Dallas, Texas. It has a great mission statement board that hangs on the walls inside the gym and hallways. It includes their values, principles, and standards.

Each time I am there, I love to stop and read it. In fact, I often buy books about a country or city I might be working or speaking in to better understand the culture and way of doing things. Knowing a few words in their language also goes a long way, I might add!

Great coaches aim to learn, understand, and respect other cultures and environments.

4. Great coaches adapt to the age or level of the athlete.

What if I told you that I know a coach who has worked with over four Olympic champions and athletes ranked in the top 10 in the world in their sport, but he has never developed or worked with an athlete under the age of 16? Would you believe me? Well it's true! This guy is a great coach, but great for only that level. In fact, he called me one Saturday morning to ask what he could do with a friend's 10-year-old son who had come to his club to practice. You see, we tend to think that the best coaches are complete. That is not always the case. A great coach is someone who understands the whole picture.

When I refer to the whole picture, I am talking about a coach understanding and having experience in developing an athlete through the LTAD (Long Term Athlete Development) plan — a coach who has worked with kids through the different stages, from say eight years of age and upwards. I tell coaches to avoid getting stuck in one age group or level at first, but rather gain as much knowledge and experience working with all age groups and levels to understand the psychological challenges and physical changes in a child. A great coach understands how to develop the whole athlete, from toddler to adult. Great coaches understand what and how much a child can do at a certain age and stage. They understand and adapt to what is needed to develop the child in a healthy and positive manner.

Equip athletes for life, not just for a sport.

Many people think the best coaches today are the ones they see on television or read about in the daily sports pages. Here's what I've also discovered: Some of the best coaches and best training environments are people and places you and I might never see or hear of. I have conducted children's clinics in far away places, like the Australian Outback and places in South Africa, and I can tell you the energy and quality of coaching has been way better than some of the high profile academies and clubs that term themselves as 'high performance'.

We need to remember that **a great environment has nothing to do with fancy equipment or facilities, but more to do with people and standards.**

Coach K

One of the best examples of a coach who understands the importance of adapting and adjusting is Coach Mike Krzyzewski, better known as 'Coach K.' Since 1980, Coach K has served as head coach of the men's basketball team at Duke University. At Duke, Krzyzewski has led his team to five NCAA championships, 12 Final Fours, 12 ACC regular season titles, and 13 ACC tournament championships. He is also the coach of the United States men's national basketball team, winners of two gold medals at the 2008 Summer Olympics and 2012 Summer Olympics. He was also an assistant coach for the 1992 "Dream Team."

I have always been a great admirer of Coach K. I recently purchased and listened to his audiobook entitled, *The Gold Standard.* In one chapter of the book, he talks about being elected as a college coach to head up the national men's Olympic team, which included some big NBA superstars like Lebron James, Jason Kidd, Kobe Bryant, and Carmelo Anthony. Coach K was chosen above all the NBA coaches, which is a very unique achievement since he had come from a college setting and background.

But besides Coach K's impressive college basketball resume, one of the main reasons he was chosen was because of his ability to bring individuals together and play as one. However, his real personal strength came from the fact that he was able to adapt and adjust to whoever he was coaching, whether an NBA superstar or a freshman straight out of high school.

"To coach and lead others is a great opportunity, but to be successful over the long haul, you have to adapt and adjust. That is the key to success."

- Coach K

Coach K is respected by his peers as one of the greatest coaches of all time, not just because of his total wins or his national championships, but because he has maintained success for such an extended period and won with such dramatically different approaches to the game throughout the years.

In his words: *"Sometimes when people ask what adjustments I've had to make over the years, they make it sound as if I've had to do something hard,"* he says. *"I think a lot of the things are easier to do if you are a willing learner. You have to be willing to learn what's best and then adjust, because every year is different, every team is different. So you should want to be in a constant state of making adjustments. The most incredibly interesting thing about being a leader is what adjustments you make and how you make them while keeping your core principles alive and well."*

Coach K says that when others ask for his advice on adapting as a leader, he has two suggestions: **Get to know those you are leading and learn to communicate in a way they can understand.**

"Look at your team," he says. *"Do you have a veteran group, or do you have a young group? What is their attention span? What is the culture that they are coming from? It is up to you as the communicator to know who you are addressing. It is not like some special science. It's wanting to learn more about people and really knowing the people you are leading at that point. And not making those people fit into something that you did in the past. You have to create an environment for those people, for the people that you have right now."*

The way he gets to know his athletes and how to reach each one has changed greatly over the years, largely because college basketball's relationship with the NBA has evolved. Again, he's learned to adapt. Great coaches expect the unexpected. They don't get flustered by sudden changes or surprises. They have a mindset of looking for a solution, and not dwelling on the problems.

Great coaches have a mindset of looking for solutions instead of dwelling on problems.

"The ability to adapt is everything"

- Denis Waitley

2. Understanding the Generation You are Working with.

This is the area where I feel that the future great coach will be ahead of the game and his peers. The great coach understands that the key to successful coaching is in relationships and connecting with others. It is imperative to him/her to have a deeper understanding of those he/she is working with.

One thing I try to do is keep up-to-date with the current trends that today's youth are interested in. For example, their music, their social media, and especially their style and methods of communication. Personally, I have a few social media accounts, such as Facebook and Twitter. One thing I've discovered is that I can find out the results of my athletes' matches or competitions faster just by reading their Facebook or Twitter accounts! I have come to understand that today's generation would rather text than talk on the phone. I don't get upset or see it as disrespectful even though I did it a different way growing up. I simply learned how this generation communicates and functions.

It's a different generation we're dealing with today, and as coaches we have to adapt and deal with it in a different way. The Internet has changed everything — the way we think, socialize, interact, communicate, and even order food! We need to understand that today's generation, the millennial generation, wants information instantly. This is also a generation that doesn't like to listen to long lectures or read self-help books.

Again, I have often surprised my students and younger athletes by being able to name certain songs from the music groups or artists they follow, or being able to talk about current trends. This is a huge part of a coach's success, because if you can't connect to the athlete as a person first, you miss the essence and value of what coaching is all about. It's about people first, then the athlete.

The great coach understands that the key to successful coaching is in relationships and connecting with others.

A great book I mentioned earlier is Tim Elmore's *Generation iY.* The iY Generation are the millennials born after 1990. In his book he describes how their world has been defined by technology and shaped by the Internet — iPod, iBook, iPhone, iChat, iMovie, iPad, and iTunes — and for many of them, life is pretty much about "I." They are a group who desires to change the world, but they just don't have what it takes to accomplish their lofty dreams, because when the work becomes difficult, they change their minds and move on to something else. Elmore argues that we need to change the way we interact with them, so that they can grow into adulthood and be the leaders they need to be.

This generation of children and young adults desperately needs mentors. Again, this is the reason why I believe that a great coach or teacher must have great values, standards, and principles in order to lead.

To me, a great coach is not determined on trophies or championships, but on how many lives he or she has influenced for the better. It's about making athletes better people. An athletic career can be short, but a life can extend many years. **Equip athletes for life, not just for a sport.**

This generation wants information quickly and in short bouts.

Today's youth don't want to be lectured or preached to. This generation grows and learns through participation. They also prefer short bits of information or messages rather than long lectures or stories.

We don't need to look any further than today's most popular social media sources like Twitter, Facebook, Snapchat, Instagram, etc., to see why they are so widely used. The reason is that this generation wants information quickly and in short bouts. This is how we need to coach and teach them. There is nothing worse than hearing a coach give long speeches or lectures on a court or field to a group of teenagers or young kids. After five minutes, that message gets lost.

According to an article by Ian Jukes, *Understanding the Digital Generation: Teaching and Learning in the New Digital Landscape,* more than 60 percent of students today are visual or visual kinesthetic learners. Yet many educators and coaches still stand in front of a classroom or training group lecturing for the duration of a class or practice session even though the new digital generation of learners prefers learning that is relevant, active, instantly useful, and fun. The digital generation students prefer to be engaged and discover more content through exploration, interaction, and collaboration, rather than non-digital generation students who may prefer being lectured. In other words it's a 'learn by doing generation, not a 'learn by lecturing or telling generation.'

These are examples that coaches need to take into serious consideration when working with the new generation: knowing how they learn, receive information, and function.

The question is: What will the next generation bring? One thing is for certain, if coaches don't keep up-to-date and stay connected, they will struggle to effectively coach and connect with them. So my question to you is: How much time are you willing to invest in this area? All the knowledge in the world won't help if you can't communicate in an understanding way with the generation you are working with.

Your ability to communicate with young people will determine your success.

- Jim Harrick

3. Understanding the Athletes Learning Style.

Relative to the above section on adapting to different generations and the way they receive information, it's important to understand how athletes learn. In my career I have noticed that certain athletes understand instructions immediately, while others take a while for information to process. If you're involved in coaching, this is something I'm sure you've had to deal with on numerous occasions. Some coaches become impatient with athletes who don't get it as quickly as others. You might think that athletes who don't understand an instruction or how to do certain skills as quickly as the next person, aren't 'smart.' It is more likely that they just don't understand because of the way you have instructed them. On many occasions I have worked with some incredibly bright and intellectual athletes who have attended Ivy League schools here in the United States, such as Harvard or Princeton, who don't always get it instantaneously. I often hear coaches complain about the fact that a certain kid in their group is slow, or doesn't 'get it' like the others. The fact that an athlete doesn't understand or 'get it' right away does not reflect on his/her level of intelligence. As a coach you need to be able to adapt to how they learn.

The fact that an athlete doesn't understand or 'get it' straight away doesn't have a reflection on their level of intelligence.

So far I have mentioned the fact that athletes are all different and come in many shapes and forms. The same goes for us coaches. In Chapter 2, I spoke about having a certain method of coaching and the way you communicate with your athlete, but it is important to understand that to be a great coach, you need to be able to adapt and adjust to the way the athlete or individual learns best. What really matters is not what is being said, but what is being understood.

What really matters is not what is being said, but rather what is being understood.

So why do we need to adapt our teaching styles? By knowing the athletes' learning styles, it helps with assisting the coach in preparing players and teams to reach their maximum potential. By understanding individual learning styles, coaches may be better able to maximize their athletes' performances. Simply put, a learning style is a preferred way of taking in and processing information in order to develop knowledge and skill.

The way the coach presents information and feedback impacts the athlete's ability to understand new concepts and acquire new skills and techniques. As such, a key effectiveness strategy for coaches who wish to create a learning relationship that accelerates learning in the athletic domain is to gain a greater understanding of their athletes' learning styles. I believe that great coaches have the ability to adapt and adjust to how they "teach" to suit the individual needs of athletes.

"If a child can't learn the way we teach, maybe we should teach the way they learn."

- Ignacio Estrada

While I believe that your older athletes (teens or older) should have a basic understanding of how they learn best, in reality, most athletes have very little knowledge about their learning style. Coaches who know the different learning style preferences are able to include every style in their practice sessions, thereby meeting the needs of the entire athlete group. By paying careful attention to the design of practice and providing opportunities to learn for all types of learners, coaches will increase the likelihood that all of their athletes are striving to reach their potential.

So What are the Different Learning Styles?

There are three distinct types of learning styles, better known as the 'VAK' (Visual-Auditory-Kinesthetic) learning. As a coach you should know these learning styles and identify early on which style works best for your athletes.

Visual Learners

I like to call these learners the '**lookers**,' not because of their appearance, but because of the way they visualize to learn. Visual learners' primary source of information is received through their eyes. The visual learner learns best by watching a demonstration or model. Seeing another athlete demonstrate a movement, noting visual cues that reinforce key concepts of skill performance, and looking for visual reference points, are helpful tools for the enhancement of learning. Coaches using visual aids to supplement their instruction, feedback, and discussions will enhance the visual learning athlete's ability to process information. Studying pictures, analyzing videotape, viewing charts, and accessing diagrams are all useful tools to enhance the learning process of visual learning athletes.

Auditory Learners

I like to call these learners the '**ear specialists**.' Auditory learners learn best through the use of language, including lectures, group discussions and audiotapes. To enhance understanding of athletes who are auditory learners, coaches should provide opportunities for athletes to talk through plays, movements, skill cues, and game strategies with other team members and/or coaches. Coaches can also videotape team talks, instructional cues, and keys to enhanced performance so that their auditory learners can listen repeatedly over time.

Kinesthetic Learners

I like to call these learners the "**doers**." Kinesthetic learners learn by doing. Information is actually processed and learned when the performer is provided an opportunity to move. Coaches have historically been instructed to get their players into 'game like' situations as soon as possible. All learners have a need to touch things and try their new skills. But the athlete who is a kinesthetic learner needs to know what the movement feels like. They need to be physically taken through the specific skill to learn and understand it better.

From my experience as a coach, I like to incorporate all three of the above learning styles. Great coaches are also great demonstrators. They are able to explain and demonstrate to the athlete how something should be performed or executed. In my workshops I often advise coaches to practice the skills and drills they show their athletes.

When coaches better themselves in the way they teach and execute a message, they automatically better their athletes.

The lookers, ear specialists and the doers.

Speaking the different industry languages.

Do you speak 'athlete', 'coach' or 'physio?' What do I mean here? Well, I believe that to be able to work effectively with all the team/staff members (athletes, coaches, doctors, physiotherapists, etc.) in a sport, you need to be able to speak a bit of their language. I'm not talking about their native language (which of course does help tremendously!), but rather it's important to adapt to the way their tribe talks and the jargon they use in their sector or industry.

Especially in the professional sports industry, you cannot be taken seriously if you don't understand and speak a certain amount of the language in the specific sport you are working in. For example, if I am going to work with a group of squash players, I should know what a 'drive,' 'let,' or a 'nick' is. If I am working with a volleyball group, I should know what a 'spike,' 'dump,' or 'dig' is. Before any coaching session with a group of athletes, I will always do my research and try to learn the language.

This also includes working in a team environment. For example, working in an environment where there might be doctors, physiotherapists, sports scientists, or a medical team, it's important to understand their terminology as well. I'm not saying you need to learn the whole dictionary on how a doctor or sports scientist speaks, but having some knowledge and being familiar with the terminologies they use is most helpful to all involved. They will also have a higher level of respect for you as a trainer or coach when you can speak a bit of their language.

On that note, if you don't know what something means or what it is, ask or look it up. But don't just nod your head and agree. Believe me, you will not look stupid when you ask a question. Your peers will respect you for your honesty and willingness to learn.

A great coach makes an effort to learn and adapt to the language and jargon used in the different departments.

Why False Feedback Fails.

We all need feedback to improve. One area where I feel coaches are not consistent enough in, is providing feedback to the athlete or parent that is honest, regardless if it's nice or not.

In the coaching industry, they speak about the 5 to 1 ratio of giving positive feedback to negative, when dealing with athletes or kids. Personally, I go with about a 3:1 ratio, not because I'm a 'less positive' coach, but because we need to be honest, realistic, and give the right kind of feedback that improves the athlete — not feedback that keeps the parents happy.

I have been privileged to coach and work in different parts of the world, including places such as Russia, South Africa, Serbia, Australia, and of course where I am based and live now, the United States. During these times, I have been able to learn and witness the different styles in teaching methods of coaches and how they communicate to their athletes and kids.

One thing that stands out about the Eastern European style of coaching is that they are direct, honest, and sometimes brutal in their assessments. I can tell you that here, in the US or even the UK, that kind of coaching style wouldn't be accepted by many. In the United States, it's the opposite. If you are not a 'positive' coach, then you won't last in many academies or clubs. The culture here is more about complimenting than criticizing. Where do I stand? Somewhere in between, but leaning more towards brutal honesty brought across in the right manner. Personally, I don't like to use the word *criticize*. I prefer using the term *information*. I believe that proper coaching is about providing the positives and then giving the right information.

When I share feedback with an athlete, it usually centers around these 3 things:

1. The timing of it.
2. Feedback based on the facts with proof.
3. Feedback that is honest (nice or not).

Start with the positives, then go from there.

I am not only lying to the athletes if I am not giving them the information and honest feedback they need to hear, worse, I am lying to myself. We need to remember that we should aim to be respected rather than liked. In my opinion, there is nothing more detrimental than seeing a coach or parent tell a kid they had a 'great' game, when in fact, they didn't. That's false feedback. Now, I completely understand the importance of building confidence in the athlete, but that athlete needs to know what is honestly helping his or her progress, and what isn't. Constantly shouting, "Good job," when it isn't a good job, doesn't help the athlete, and this kind of feedback fails in the long term. It simply sends a false message to the athlete or child, because after a while they don't know when they actually have done something really well or not. They begin to become skeptical of your praise.

Constantly shouting, "Good job" when it isn't a good job, doesn't help the athlete. This kind of feedback fails in the long term.

The most important kind of feedback is honest feedback — realistic and straightforward feedback that helps grow and improve the athlete or child. We need to develop the growth mindset in those we coach, not just the athlete, but the parent too. You don't improve with criticism, but rather you improve with the right kind of information. This kind of feedback is what I call *flattering feedback*, which only hurts the learning and developmental process more than it helps.

Remember that effective communication is 80 percent how it is delivered and 20 percent the actual message said. One commonality of the best athletes I've worked with is that they all handle feedback and criticism (information) well. In most cases, their upbringing mirrors this quality from the way their parents and teachers have offered it.

In conclusion, great coaches adapt like chameleons. They adjust well to those they are working with. They understand that to be effective, they need to 'dial' into those they work with. They are also in touch and tune with today's generation.

Coach Time

1. *As a coach, what changes do you feel you need to make in order to progress?*

2. *What do you find is the biggest challenge in working with today's generation of kids?*

3. *Do you see your more 'difficult' athletes as a great challenge to improve your coaching and communication skills or something you would rather pass along?*

4. *How good are you at adapting to the unexpected or things changing without notice?*

5. *Do you demonstrate a good example of self-control to your athletes when the unexpected occurs?*

6. *In what areas do you feel you could do better in when it comes to adapting?*

CHAPTER 4

Energy

Your energy introduces you well before you speak!

– Anon

Maybe this resonates with you. I find that there are people and places that make me feel like I'm building my energy stores, that rejuvenate me, and help me to do my best work. This is when I notice that all my 'coaching powers' begin to surge. I am in a place where I feel I can do my best work. In fact, I think it is the outcome of the working environments we choose that are a big factor in determining how we feel and how productive we can be. We need to remember that environments are more about people than just buildings or structures.

Likewise, there are people and places that suck my energy, leaving me exhausted. This bothers me because it steals the energy that I could be giving to someone who really deserves it. I have always said that I would happily train an athlete who might be the worst in the group athletically or technically, but has a great work ethic, than be with the most talented athlete who has a bad attitude, poor work ethic, or negative energy. In the same manner, I would rather work alongside a coach with minimum experience but a great energy and drive, than an experienced coach who is unmotivated and has a poor energy. This is a message I especially try to convey to the younger new coaches out there: your energy and attitude will get you a lot further than your certificates and coaching badges.

Your energy and attitude will get you further than your certificates and coaching badges.

In my experience, I have found that the best coaches out there are not the most knowledgeable or experienced ones, but rather the ones who exude a great energy and can motivate others best. They have a unique way of making you feel motivated, energized, and inspired. These coaches are the energy givers.

In this chapter we look at three distinct areas that contribute to having a great energy in coaching:

1. Your Personal Energy

2. Motivation

3. The Energy Business

1. Your Personal Energy

We are all attracted to people who have a great energy. Let's face it, none of us wants to hang around a negative Nancy or a moaning Mike. **I believe that there are two kinds of people in this world, the energy providers or givers, and the energy vampires.** We will go into this in more detail later in this chapter.

Great coaches have an aura about them. They are positive, optimistic, and just fun to be around, even though they take their work extremely seriously. Just like you and I prefer to be around these kinds of people, so too do your athletes and clients enjoy being around a positive and enthusiastic coach.

'Aura' definition: "An ever changing flow of life around one's body"

I believe that in life your energy is everything. Energy is powerful enough to create your own success or contribute to your decline. Everything you are involved in is a result of the energy you contribute. As a coach you may have all the experience, knowledge, and skills, but if you have poor energy or attitude, you will find the coaching industry an unrewarding and unsatisfying one. Never forget that we attract and become what we hold in our minds both consciously and subconsciously.

Several times a year I do presentations on this subject for coaches' workshops and conferences, as well as for corporate companies around the world. I stress the fact that everything involves energy, and that a healthier and more energetic you, results in more productivity in the work place, as well as more happiness and success in life.

We attract and become what we hold in our minds both consciously and subconsciously.

We need to understand that we owe our athletes and clients the best form of ourselves. We need to be consistent from sun-up to sundown. We can't start out great in the morning only to run flat like a battery, dropping our level of focus and commitment the longer the day goes on. It is our responsibility as coaches and trainers to have positive energy every day for each and every athlete and client.

So what contributes to having a good energy? I've listed 8 factors below that I feel are essential:

1. Your Attitude (yes, it all starts here!)

2. Your Lifestyle.

3. Your quality of Sleep.

4. Your Nutrition and hydration habits.

5. Exercise.

6. Your daily habits and routines.

7. Your relationships and those you associate with.

8. Being grateful.

To give others energy, you first need to have it yourself.

I have always believed that to be able to give and provide others with a great energy, we need to first have it ourselves. We need to understand that as coaches, we are in the service and energy business.

Just like our athletes, as coaches we are reliant on our health and wellness to perform. Coaching is a profession that can drain you both physically and mentally. The great coach understands that there are no 'set times' in this industry. When we are working early mornings, and sometimes late into the evenings or weekends, it definitely takes a toll. This is where making ourselves a priority and taking steps to better care for ourselves are so important. Our performance and quality of work as coaches are reliant on how well we take care of ourselves. Just like an elite athlete aims to perform at his or her peak, we, too, need to put in the daily effort and work to improve.

At the upper level of professional sport, we have often seen high profile coaches fall ill from being overworked and over stressed. An article I read a few months back described how Australian AFL coaches experienced high levels of stress from their increasingly demanding jobs, some becoming seriously ill at certain stages of the season. Top level coaching can be a demanding job, which sometimes involves a lot of pressure and long working hours. A study by Dr. Marte Bentzen, which is featured on the *Norwegian School of Sports Science* website, found that as many as one in four coaches feel a high level of fatigue that leads to burn-out. In my opinion, I would say that figure is more. We need to understand that taking care of ourselves should be our biggest priority, not just from a career perspective.

Those who don't have time for health and wellness now, will have to find time for illness and injury later.

Five Strategies to Give You More Energy

1. Develop good habits and routines.

Just like the best athletes have developed performance winning habits over time, so too should you develop winning habits as a coach and person.

Some of the most successful business people and athletes I have met or worked with, all have great habits. For example, they are great with time management, they get up early, and they are always well prepared for their business meetings or practices. To create a great energy, your daily habits play a significant role in this, like what you eat, how you prepare for the day, when you exercise, how much you hydrate during the day, etc.

I personally have set routines and habits I have built into my day that include:

• Writing down my priorities (no more than 2-3 things)

- Things to do (includes appointments, athletes, etc.)
- Exercise/stretching
- Thoughtfulness
- Reading
- Nutrition — set meal times
- Hydration — drinking at least eight glasses of water per day
- Nap time
- Protein intake every four hours
- Emailing and returning phone calls

Over time I have been able to develop these routines and habits into my life, which have helped me tremendously. I have seen incredible results all around. If you want to make changes in your life and wellness, you need to put time aside each day and commit to it, because the most important appointment of the day should be with yourself.

The most important appointment of the day is with yourself.

One of my all time favorite quotes was on the wall of a certain university training room. It said: *"Champions do not become champions on the court. They are merely recognized on the court. They become champions in their daily routine. Players do not decide their future. They decide their habits, then their habits decide their future."* I believe this applies to all of us. Our habits decide who we become.

Change your habits, change your life.

Start Small

When it comes to developing routines, start small. Focus on establishing just one simple routine in your life, and give yourself a month to do it. For example, you could set 20 minutes aside each morning to stretch or read. Instead of establishing an elaborate daily routine, pick a very small block of time to devote each day to your routine. Instead of multiple activities, focus on just one activity. Spend some time thinking about the single, simple routine you want to establish. A good starting routine is one that is simple, one that involves something you would have to do anyway. As you get into developing this first routine, you can then start establishing the next routine.

Another trick is to leave yourself effective reminders. For example, write on sticky notes and leave them around the house or working place. Sometimes I will have messages and reminders on my phone screen saver to help me develop new habits. At the moment mine says: *"Keep hydrating, keep snacking, keep smiling."*

The most common problem that many people have with establishing new routines is simply remembering to do them at the appropriate time. So, like I mentioned, it's important to write things down and see them throughout the day. This is how you effectively develop great habits and routines, one at a time.

The secret to change is to focus all your energy on building the new, not on fighting the old.

2. Exercise and Stretch daily.

One of the keys to obtaining great energy is exercising. A lot of coaches tend to think they are 'healthy' or 'fit' just because they are involved in the sports industry. Nothing could be further from the truth. As coaches we put others first, which means that our own needs are put on the back burner. This is what I preach to coaches and trainers who attend my workshops: **It's you that matters most. To give energy to others, you first have to have the energy and vitality yourself.** World class tennis coach Magnus Norman wrote a great piece in his blog entitled, *"Please put on your own mask before helping others,"* meaning, you first have to take care of yourself before helping others.

I hear coaches complain about how sore they are or how many hip surgeries or knee replacements they have had, but when you ask them what they do regarding their own exercise and well being, most mumble "not much." Being healthy requires action. It requires that you make the effort to make the changes. Working or being involved in sport doesn't make you 'fit' or 'healthy.' You need to set that time aside, make it a habit, and purposefully have a plan.

Coaching involves demonstrating certain movements and exercises. A healthier coach will be able to perform these tasks better.

Just 20 minutes a day can make a world of difference in how you will feel. Some stretches, foam rolling, and a few strength exercises can change the way you feel and how much energy you will have! It's about making it a priority in your daily routine and sticking to it.

The most energetic and dynamic coaches I've met all love to exercise and keep healthy. In the early morning when I'm out running or at the gym during a Grand Slam, I usually see the same people. These coaches are up before their athletes and before their working day starts. Remember, as coaches, we need to set the example and walk the talk.

It's about making it a priority in your daily routine and sticking to it.

3. Prepare your meals for the week.

Here's a big one! Let me start with this: I believe that two thirds of our physical appearance is due to nutrition. The quality (or lack) of our daily eating habits determines how we look, feel, and think. As coaches we sometimes have schedules where we are all over the place and suddenly realize we haven't hydrated or eaten in hours. Just like an athlete, this affects our own performance.

The best way to eat healthier and have the right foods on hand is setting aside time to prepare your meals for the week ahead. For example, I allocate time every Sunday afternoon to do my grocery shopping and prepare my meals for the week. I make sure I buy an array of healthy snacks that are easy to take with me when I'm on the run or traveling. I also make sure I carry protein powder and a shaker bottle so I can ingest protein every four hours.

Let me ask you this: Have you ever met a professional figure competitor or bodybuilder? You will notice that they always have a cooler box nearby filled with their food. They prepare their meals and have them with them throughout the day. We can all learn from this. It just requires effort and making it a habit!

Relying on vending machines or the corner store to eat healthy isn't going to work. You need to plan purposefully and have the right foods readily available throughout the day. Each morning I take five minutes to prepare my lunch bag for the day, which includes fruit, snacks, and a Tupperware container of chicken and salad. It has become a habit for me, and it makes the world of difference in how I feel and how much energy I can give to others. I also make it a habit to snack every hour and drink a glass of water.

4. Take a daytime nap.

Napping is something I have carried over from my days of competing as an athlete. I have always believed in having a nap after lunch in the middle of the day. A 20 minute nap after lunch makes a big difference in my energy later in the day. I strongly recommend to the athletes I consult and work with that they take a day nap to maximize their second practice in the afternoon. At first they don't like it, but they eventually realize how beneficial it is to their performance. Great coaching is about consistency in your performance. You can't be giving 100 percent in the morning, then only 50 percent later in the day. By taking a daytime nap, it not only helps you to switch off and recharge, but also improves your energy levels, performance, concentration and mood later on in the day.

As a coach, how can you expect to perform at a consistently high level if you don't have the energy?

5. Sleep

Let me start by confessing that I am not the world's greatest sleeper. Being a constant thinker, my mind hardly shuts down. For example, if I think of an idea at 2 a.m., I get up and write it down! However, I have realized that sleep is an essential component to my performance and energy level. You might be able to get away with five or six hours of sleep a night, but are you really maximizing your potential? Probably not.

Sleep plays a vital role in good health and well-being throughout your life. Getting enough quality sleep helps with your mental health, physical health, and quality of life. I now shut down electronics at least one hour before bedtime, like my laptop and phone (I hardly watch TV, but that would be another one). I like to read in bed until I fall asleep, which is usually around 10 p.m., as I aim for seven hours of sleep. Sleep is key for recovery and energy. To maximize optimum performance, it's important that you have a set bedtime and wake-up time that involves at least seven to nine hours of sleep per night.

Your energy is closely related to your daily lifestyle habits and routines.

Five Things Every Coach Needs to be Great:

1. Consistency

Being consistent as a coach isn't only about your work ethic and standard of coaching. It also has to do with your moods and consistency in attitude. **You, as a coach, need to be able to bring that same experience to your clients and athletes every single day.** You cannot be up one day and down the next. I repeatedly come across trainers and coaches in gyms and sports clubs who look tired or uninterested, like they just don't want to be there.

We need to understand that achieving greatness and excellence is not easy. World class coaches have an energy and enthusiasm that is contagious. Their attention to detail and level of understanding about the sport, the team, each individual player and staff member, comes from spending more time working on being the best of the best. They understand that to be consistent, they need to be able to maintain standards even when fatigued and under pressure. They expect and insist on quality, detail, and intensity in preparation.

To be respected as a great coach, you need to be consistent in your moods and the way you interact with people. Saying 'hi' one day and then walking past a person the next day is not consistent. And while I'm on that subject . . . if only coaches and trainers realized the power of saying a simple consistent "hello" to people they see each day. What I have noticed is that coaches or trainers only greet their athletes and clients, not realizing that potential clients are all around them.

Consistency requires having energy. It requires taking care of your lifestyle and being able to pace yourself to be able to perform at a high standard. A great coach is consistent in behavior, work ethic, time management, communication, values, and standards. Coaches inspire not just with words, but in the action, consistency, passion, and professionalism that they demonstrate in all they do.

2. Sustainability

It's important to understand that to be effective and consistent in this field, we need to be realistic in the standards, values, and work ethic we represent. A good example of this is having an ideal job or position while working in a positive environment with great athletes and clients to train. But let's say you are forced to commute an hour and a half with added traffic problems along the way. At first you might be able to tolerate it, but over the long run it will not be sustainable. The days, weeks, and months will begin to add up and take their toll on you. The stress will contribute to your 'energy loss.' Or, as we see in some cases, coaches might work early mornings and later into the evenings due to the possibility of 'peak hours' and more business. But the effect it eventually has on your significant others, your lifestyle, moods, and energy is detrimental. There is no way you can expect to sustain and perform in the long run. You need to be sustainable as a person. At the end of the day, it is your personal leadership and energy that people are counting on.

3. (Im)Balance

Here is an area that sometimes creates a little controversy. But the fact is, if you want to be great in something, you need to do what others are not willing to do. **'Normal' doesn't create excellence.**

There is no such thing as having a 'balance' when you are trying to maximize your potential as a coach, or anything else for that matter. Where there are priorities there are imbalances. There are limits, yes, but when it comes to balance, you must accept that you are in a profession that requires long hours, sometimes giving up your weekends and holidays. There is much written about balance, but in my observation, most of the great coaches I've worked with have little to none. You see, the great coaches are always looking for ways to better themselves. They seem to never switch off, as they are always looking for better ways to do things and get the best from their athletes.

However, we have seen how coaches are able to have some control in the balance of spending time with loved ones and family. We know that Coach K travels with his family most of the time, as well as many other coaches in the league. Any great coach who has reached a high level has probably spent a great deal of time away from home and loved ones. Unfortunately, sometimes this is what it takes. Personally, I would say I've spent between 200-250 days per year away from home in the last 8-10 years while working with professional athletes on the tour.

'The One Thing', a book by Gary Keller and Jay Papasan, states that 'balance is bunk.' A balanced life is a lie. Why? Because you will always put your priorities first. In other words, **whatever is most important to you will be given the majority of your energy and time**. To achieve extraordinary results in anything, we are required to spend more time in these areas. And like it or not, this demands getting out of balance.

Pursuing anything worth having is about imbalances. No great coach gets there by doing 'just enough.' However, our challenge to become great at what we do involves the control of these imbalances. Being a great coach does require a certain amount of sacrifice, but the challenge is in how we can have 'some' balance.

No one who reached a high level in anything got there by being 'normal' or doing 'just enough.'

4. Confidence in Yourself

Let me start with this question: Would you feel happy to be led by a boss, manager, or coach who wasn't confident in him or herself?" Of course not! We all seek confident leaders.

Great coaches are confident in themselves. They thrive on helping others feel the same. Just like our athletes, every coach is different and unique. We all have different strengths and limitations. It is in this uniqueness and daring to be different that sets the great coaches apart from the rest. **Great coaches are not afraid to try new things, be creative, and stretch their thinking.** Great coaches do it their way. They learn from other great coaches. They know that being the best means not being afraid to question things and sometimes do them differently. Great coaches have the confidence to develop identities and methods in their coaching while maintaining high standards. They lead from the front and give confidence to those they train.

5. Belief in Yourself

To lead you need to have a strong belief in yourself. Your athletes need to see that you believe in your methods and what you are teaching them to do. As a coach, your beliefs provide your athletes with a sense of security. Great coaches believe in themselves and back themselves.

The coaching world can be a very critical one with a lot of knocking each others' training methods and philosophies down. **Great coaches possess a belief that is able to withstand negatives, setbacks, obstacles, and failures.** They believe in their methods and their coaching abilities. Like they say, *"If you don't believe in yourself, nobody else will."*

Here's three things that I promise will increase your energy, as well as improve your happiness, success rate, and income

1. Be nice.

2. Smile more

3. Say 'hello' to people first.

Not that difficult, is it?

Do you always say hello to everyone?

December 13th, 2015, Inspire Football Coaches Conference, London England

I was invited to speak at the Inspire Football Conference in London by Jon Trew last year. Jon is one of the nicest guys in the business and has a passion for developing coaches. The Inspire Coaches Conference is where some of the smartest minds in football coaching attend. Entering the building, I proceeded to the reception area of the London Business School and asked for the location of the conference room where I would be speaking. The lady behind the counter said she was going there anyway, and I could go with her. Walking through the hallways and lounge areas I greeted and said *"hello"* to people as I walked through. As we were entering the conference room, the lady turned to me and asked: *"Do you say 'hello' to everyone?"* To which I smiled and replied: *"I must do."* In all honesty, I hadn't realized that I had made saying hello to strangers a habit. I'm glad I do it, because sometimes you might walk past a person you may have met before, and if you didn't say 'Hi," they might think you either forgot them or you are just being unfriendly. Anyway, it's just a habit that I'm happy I have developed.

Pace yourself.

Just like running a marathon, you need to be able to pace yourself as a coach. I remember starting out as a 20-year-old personal trainer back in Johannesburg, South Africa. I would be up at 4 a.m. putting in my first training bike ride out on the road, then heading to work by 5.30 a.m. to see my first client, break for lunch to train again, then see clients sometimes until 9 p.m. I did this for maybe seven or eight years. Now a little older (and maybe slower), I need to be wiser about how I pace myself and plan my days. Regrettably, over the last two or three years, I've had to decline some speaking and presentation opportunities due to a better understanding of my body and energy levels. I understand better now than I did when I was in my 20s, that it's a marathon, not a sprint. I realize I am blessed to be in this position, but sometimes you have to say 'No.'

Okay, I know what you are probably thinking — here's a guy who in 2013 took over 90 flights and ran 12 marathons in 12 months, then 7 marathons in 7 weeks, and he's telling me about 'pacing?' I can tell you that the running part was not the challenge, but rather the planning, nutrition, sleep, recovery, flights, and work. It just shows when you plan and prepare carefully, it's all possible!

Today, I have structured and designed my habits and daily routines around being able to have a great energy experience all day. This includes set wake-up times, set bedtimes, better nutrition, exercise and stretching, a day time nap, switching off electronics, allowing time to spend with my significant others, etc. Having developed these simple routines and habits into my day, I can honestly say that I have seen for myself the massive differences in my attitude, knowledge, energy, performance, and relationships. **Nobody can tell me they don't have 20 minutes a day to exercise and stretch. You are obviously not making yourself a priority if you can't make this time. Remember, it's not about finding the time, but rather making the time.** Just like you meticulously plan your athletes' season and programs, so too should you plan your own lifestyle and wellness program.

Just like you so carefully and meticulously plan your athletes' training programs, so too, should you plan your own lifestyle and wellness program.

Walking the Talk

Something I strongly believe in is that if you are working in the sport, health or fitness industry, you should walk the talk. You cannot look out of shape and exhausted half the time if you are seeking respect from your clients and athletes. We don't need to be running marathons or entering Ironman's to gain respect, we simply need to just make an effort on taking care of ourselves better. Now, this is by no means an attack or judgment on others, but let me ask you this: Would you go to a dentist with bad teeth? Or how about going to a mechanic whose own car is always breaking down? We are in the 'health and energy' business. We need to live it, promote it, drive it, be it.

I remember a story from my days working for a Dutch National Sports Federation back in 2005. On this particular day, a coach who worked there was giving a group of kids between the ages of 12 and 14 a talk, or should I say, lecture, on nutrition. The problem was that this particular coach was about 50 lbs. overweight and the kids knew he enjoyed indulging in food and treats. Needless to say, the talk didn't digest too well with the kids. I repeat, I am not judging here, all I am simply stating is that your athletes (especially kids) will follow your actions rather than listen to your words. You don't need to look like a chiselled athlete or have the body of a Hollywood star to gain respect. All I am saying is that it's important for us as coaches to make an effort and take care of our appearance and ourselves. We need to remember that our example is the most powerful message.

As coaches, we need to be the example if we want to effectively lead people.

Having a Great Sense of Humor is a Great Energy Tool and Coaching Technique.

Having a great sense of humor around athletes within a team environment is, in my opinion, one of the most undervalued, but most powerful tools in bringing people together, releasing tension and stress, and having fun. Especially in the competitive environment, it is a great tool in helping an athlete feel more relaxed and less nervous. Over time we have seen many great leaders use their sense of humor in good times and bad. These include, Abraham Lincoln, Winston Churchill, John F. Kennedy, Ronald Reagan, and George W. Bush. As a coach, not taking yourself too seriously certainly helps release tension and shows your athletes that you have confidence in them.

I've been fortunate to have worked alongside some incredibly funny coaches throughout my career, people like Karel Mouton, who was the head coach to the Rand Afrikaans University cricket team, then the South African National Club Cricket Champions. Karel had a great balance of sometimes joking, but serious when needed. He knew how to keep a great energy going in the team through his sense of humor and personality. We always had to be on the lookout, as we were never too far away from being pranked.

Scientific studies have shown that moods are contagious and can be motivational. Seeing the humor in situations creates positive feelings. Positive moods generate positive actions. Negative moods generate doubt and negative actions (or inaction). My track and field coach whilst growing up, was so much fun to be around. Mr. Reynecke always made practice fun, and as a group we would always laugh and tease each other in a good way. He had a great way of making us feel confident and taking our minds off the race inadvertently, getting rid of the butterflies in our stomachs!

Too much seriousness as a coach can make your athletes feel nervous and anxious. **Great coaches have a way of distracting their athletes, making them feel relaxed and energised.** Having a great sense of humor helps tremendously with this.

Sometimes under pressure situations, a sense of humor or being funny can be a 'genius' coaching strategy.

Put on Your Own Mask before Helping Others.

Swedish tennis coach, Magnus Norman, is a good friend of mine. Magnus is a former world no. 2 tennis player and now world-class coach of many top players, including 2-time Grand Slam Champion Stan Wawrinka. I often share some training runs when we are at the Grand Slam tournaments, and I enjoy my time with him immensely. Magnus wrote a great piece on his blog (magnusnorman.com) about needing to take care of yourself first if you want to take care of others.

Magnus Norman blog (Feb, 2016):

I'm back in Sweden again after a few weeks in Australia. I love traveling. I could not live without it, as it runs in my blood from a very young age. One of the best things with traveling, however, is coming home after a few weeks on the road. I really appreciate what I have at home more when I travel. Sounds weird, right? But that's a fact for me. I love the changes in life. I never think I will be able to stay at the same place forever without moving. I love the different cultures, the struggles, meeting new people, as well as seeing new places. But to come home these days gives me a huge satisfaction and a calmness.

My priorities when I'm home these days are my two kids and my family. For a few years I didn't really make those priorities, and I wasn't really feeling great about it. I was always putting myself last. I had no energy left in my tank for friends and my family. I gained weight as a result of not living a healthy, sustainable life. I felt that I needed to change my habits a bit in order to be able to keep doing what I have been doing over time. Today my priority when I'm home is my family and my own health and well being. I'm proud about the changes I made. It has made me realize that it increased my chances to keep doing what I'm doing, with sustained energy, for a much longer time. Just the luxury to be able to drop off and collect the kids from kindergarten is amazing and gives me so much in return. I feel like I'm a better father and a better person to be around for Linda at home, and I hope I can have the possibility of working with athletes and player development for as long as I physically and mentally can. I will, however, always make sure I have a little time for my own well being as well.

I'm also very blessed to have a great team around me, as well as a great player that really cares about his team. Exactly a year ago, as an example, I had a few weeks off and took my family on a trip to catch up on time together. It was extremely valuable for us as a family. However, not all players are like that. Not many people care about the coaches and how they are holding up. Many coaches work long hours. Weekends. Early mornings. Late nights. And they get almost zero credit. Especially working with younger players. My advice is to think about your health in the first place. Before everything else. Even if it's just for a little while every day, I encourage you to make that investment for your career. You will be a better coach and you will be able to give more to your players for a longer period of time. And you will feel better on top of everything!

It's a little bit like the flight attendants who instruct us on the airplanes before take-off who tell us. . . In case of an emergency landing, *"Please put on your own mask before helping others."*

Our energy, health, and well-being are key attributes to the quality and consistency we bring to those we coach and teach.

2. Motivation

Great coaches are great motivators. In fact, motivation is probably one of the main reasons why an athlete will want to hire you as a coach or mentor. I believe that if you cannot motivate people, you cannot lead them. Earlier in the book, you might remember that I spoke about the fact that coaching was 80 percent interpersonal skills and 20 percent knowledge and coaching skills. Being a great motivator who can inspire others is a large portion of that 80 percent.

Great motivators and coaches generate trust through leading by example or "modeling the way" according to James Kouzes and Barry Posner, noted authorities on leadership.

Good motivators are also good sales people. You have to sell your athletes on hard work and the pursuit of excellence. You have to get them to buy that their hard work and sweat are worth the price of the goal. This means that you have to explain to them the necessity of their efforts. Simply telling an athlete to do something is nowhere near as effective as explaining to them how this exercise or drill will help them get closer to where they want to go.

Great coaches are great motivators.

A great coach is like a radio DJ.

To be a great motivator of others, you need to have a great energy about you. I always like to compare a great coach to that of a radio DJ. A radio DJ has to go to work every day feeling pumped and ready to bring his/her best. Let's face it, if you switch on the radio and hear a DJ sounding depressed or speaking with a boring monotone voice, you are probably going to switch to another station, right? We want to feel energized and inspired, and the same goes for those we train and coach. A great coach is like a radio DJ. He or she makes you feel motivated, uplifted, and ready to take on the day.

While waiting in the US Open players locker room with the player I was working with at that time, Alex Bogomolov , I had a quick chat with Gebhard Gritsch, who is the long time fitness trainer to world number one tennis player, Novak Djokovic. We were speaking about the dynamics within the Djokovic team, to which he said, *"Novak's coach Marian Vajda is a very positive person who is great at motivating and creating a very good energy within the team."*

A great coach is like a radio DJ. They leave their problems at home and bring energy to their show!

Motivation is such a powerful tool. It's what fuels a desire and perseverance in the athlete. However, motivation takes energy. It involves bringing it every day as a coach, and that can mentally and physically drain you. Again, this is why a big part of having energy is taking care of your own needs, such as your own nutrition, rest, and exercise. Getting the best from your athletes is about knowing and understanding what motivates them. It's about finding their *WHY.* As a coach, it's one of the first things I want to know about the athlete I am working with. Why they do it? Why they are willing to get out of bed at 4.30 a.m. to come to the gym or court? What motivates them to do this. When I can tap into that, I am giving myself the tools and the best chance as a coach to know how to get the best from them.

Below are 6 things that I believe are important factors in motivating your athletes and getting the best from them:

1. Find out what motivates them and tap into that.
2. Create an environment that motivates them.
3. Reward the right things and recognize good qualities.
4. Catch them doing the right things and tell them.
5. Provide incentives along the way.
6. Celebrate the small wins.

Don't forget to celebrate the 'small wins.'

They say that success motivates and it's true. So as coaches, we need to learn to celebrate the 'small wins' with our athletes, fellow coaches, and staff. Each day it's important to look for the small wins, like a great effort or attitude at practice, a new high score in shooting, or an athlete bettering their agility test time for example. These things, big or small, motivate people to greater things. Positive feedback is one of the best motivating factors for an athlete, and as coaches, we always need to be on the lookout for opportunities to compliment and build the athlete's confidence.

A method I use for those I coach or train is making sure we finish each practice on a positive note. I need to make sure my athlete or team is leaving on a high after practice. If an athlete is motivated and happy at the end of each practice, it's a good bet that he or she has made some progress and will be excited to come back and work even harder. This is what I term *'winning the practice'*.

Great coaches inspire and motivate others to greatness.

Your aura or personality that comes across to others has a lot to do with your ability to motivate and inspire them. Again, this is another important reason why having a consistent, positive, and uplifting attitude is important. As a coach, you can't be hot one day and cold the next.

Great coaching also comes down to setting the example yourself. **Model what you want to see — be motivated yourself.** If you want someone to work hard, you better be working hard. If you want someone to put in extra time, you better be putting in extra time. Athletes do what they see. This is why the motivation of the coaching staff is so important and why it is so important to have quality team leaders who can lead by example, hold themselves accountable, and promote a climate of motivation and inspiration. You need to set the standards by what you do, say, and expect.

You can't be 'hot' one day and 'cold' the next. You need to stay consistent in your moods.

Liverpool football club's coach, Jurgen Klopp, is a good example of a coach who has a great energy and confidence. Squad player, Divock Origi, said that Jurgen Klopp, *"Sends a lot of positive energy to everyone in the Liverpool squad. If you look at Jurgen, the immediate feeling is that he sends a lot of positive energy to everyone. He likes to work with everybody and help them make progress, and he has a clear plan. When you have a coach like this, it means you have a leader who sends this energy to the group. I think it should be a good partnership for him and Liverpool."* Just recently, Liverpool and Brazilian player, Philippe Coutinho even called Klopp the best motivator and coach he has ever worked under.

Another example of a coach with great energy and enthusiasm is NFL Football coach, Rex Ryan. Ryan is the head coach of the Buffalo Bills Football team. Eric Wood, the center for the team said, *"Rex brings a lot of energy and enthusiasm to the building on a daily basis, that's valuable."*

> ## *"Rex brings a lot of energy and enthusiasm to the building on a daily basis, that's valuable."*
>
> - Eric Wood

Whenever I speak at a coaches' seminar or workshop on this subject, I usually use the example of legendary tennis coach, Nick Bollettieri. Nick founded the Nick Bollettieri Tennis Academy in Bradenton, Florida in 1978. He went on to coach no less than ten nr. 1 players in the world, including Agassi, Becker, Courier, Hingis, Seles, Sharapova, and Venus and Serena Williams. Now well into his 80s, Nick is still going strong, rising at 4:20 every morning to get to the gym by 5:00 a.m. He starts coaching at 5:30 a.m., stopping only for a quick lunch before finishing his last lesson at 7:00 p.m.

I initially met Nick back in 2007 at the Miami Open. His warmth and smile were the first things I noticed, and I have been a great fan of his work ever since. I'm also privileged to have worked alongside Nick on many occasions with professional players. People always ask me what it is about Nick, what are the main reasons why he's been undoubtedly one of the most famous and well-known coaches in the world. It's a simple one for me to answer: *"His energy and ability to motivate players."* On many occasions I have seen world-class professional players who have been so far down in the dumps spend 15 minutes with Nick and then literally walk off the court ready to take on the world! Is it magic? No! — It's an energy and ability to motivate. Nick's ability to motivate and inspire athletes has been something that I will take with me for the rest of my coaching career. He has taught me that the power of motivation and giving others confidence is one of the main keys to being a successful coach.

Nick's qualities don't stop there, because he is a coach who truly cares about those he works with. Nick's standards and level of consistency are high, not sometimes, but all the time. This is the most powerful lesson I have probably learned in my coaching career. If you can motivate and inspire others, you will be a success.

The best coaches are the best motivators. I believe that no matter what jobs or careers these coaches go into, they would succeed due to their ability to get the best out of others. When you watch them coach, you can see that their energy is contagious, just by seeing how their athletes respond and perform.

The best coaches are the best motivators. I believe that no matter what jobs or careers these coaches would go into, they would succeed due to the ability to motivate and get the best out of others.

I believe that coaching should be a vocation, not a job. If you don't love what you do, it's hard to stay motivated. We also need to understand that motivation is a temporary thing, hence the reason why you need a consistent energy to sustain it. In fact, it's commitment that is more the long-term goal. An intrinsic motivation and love for what you do is important to stay motivated and committed. **As coaches we should be in it more for the outcome (building athletes and people), not just the income.**

If you don't love what you do, it's hard to stay motivated in the long run.

During the Indian Wells tournament in 2016, I spent the week working alongside Lleyton Hewitt, the former world no. 1 and current Australian Davis Cup team member. In his first 'official' year of coaching since he retired in Australia earlier that year, a few things are evident about Lleyton, the coach.

First, he loves the game with a deep passion. You can't hide or fake that. Secondly, he has an incredible energy that is contagious. Enjoying dinners with Lleyton and the players that week in the desert, I could feel how much the players respected him, as an athlete, a coach, and a person. That week I witnessed how he was able to connect with each player and bring a positive energy to the group. With each player there, Bernie Tomic, Nick Kyrgios and Grothy (Sam Groth), you could see how he adapted to each one's personality to get the very best from them. Let me add that all three of the above mentioned guys have completely diverse personalities.

What I respected most was that he was able to relate to an entirely different generation than what he was used to. It can't be easy being one of the game's most legendary fighters and having to coach other players who might not be willing to dig as deep as he did.

One evening before dinner, we had a 20 minute wait for our table and Lleyton decided we all go and shoot a few basketballs at the arcade next door. You can just imagine being around an incredibly competitive group of guys that it was game on! Lleyton was on fire and you could see how intense and focused he was. Small examples like this are inspiring to the players he coaches — always play to win, compete hard and lead by example, no matter what it is. On a lighter note, having won the first game against the lads that evening, I lost the last one and ended up doing push-ups inside the Cheesecake Factory restaurant that night!

In my opinion, Lleyton could coach any sport and be successful. He has the qualities to be a great coach and the energy to ignite those he leads. I'm certainly looking forward to watching him coach and hopefully work with him again over the next few years.

What really motivates great coaches?

Well, this can be different for everyone, but I have always loved the quote: *"Win the day."* This is what motivates me, leaving practice at the end of the day knowing that we (the athletes, staff and myself) won the day. 'Winning the day' is about doing the best you can do in the practices that contribute to the performance of the athlete or team. 'Winning the day' is about being focused on the process, the day-to-day efforts you put in. It's about the daily standards you have set and achieving them. Seeing others improve and succeed also motivates me.

'Winning the day' and seeing others improve motivates me.

But what motivates me might not be your main motivation. No one can deny that we all like to win. We all know that success motivates, but to me, the 'win' is in seeing others succeed and achieve things they never thought possible. When you see someone who has worked so hard to achieve something, no matter how small or insignificant it may be, that is my reward.

I recall consulting with a basketball coach in Sicily, Italy back in 2001. This particular coach was motivated solely by winning and hated to lose with a passion. Needless to say, most of the time he was on an emotional roller coaster and his players could feel it too. A coach with a ton of experience, he had a decent record with the teams he had coached. On the weekends that his team won, he was flying high, but when they lost, he was so low, he would switch his phone off and disappear for 2 days! Now in my opinion, this is an unhealthy motivation because he was being controlled by uncontrollables (outcomes). After spending a few days with him, I was able to bring the message across that, even though his passion and hunger to succeed was a factor in his success, it wasn't helping his players in the long run (or his health for that matter). Only the performance of his players was controllable, not the outcomes.

'Winning the day' is a great motivation because it keeps you in the process.

A few years back, I worked with a young girl who was a club level hockey player. She started with me when she was nine, and in all honesty, she was the worst in the group, athletically and technically. However, one thing she did have was a great work ethic and an attitude to learn and improve. This was due to having parents who understood what a healthy growth mindset was, knowing that it is not all about results and selection. To cut a long story short, after two years she was head and shoulders above the other kids in the group in all areas. Her dedication, commitment, and self-discipline, along with a great attitude, caused her to improve dramatically. These to me are the real 'wins.' The small everyday bits of hard work, together with a great attitude, made an athlete better and taught her life skills along the way. This is what motivates me!

The 'real wins' and motivation are in seeing your athletes get better each day.

Motivation and your *WHY*

Have you ever asked yourself *WHY* you coach? I'm being serious. This is an important question, because when you discover the deeper reasons for this, you then have the motivation to do better in that particular area. Is it to see others succeed? Is it to win as many championships as possible? Is it to make more money, or to develop great athletes and people?

We now understand that to coach someone to achieve their best requires us to know as much as we can about them and especially what motivates them. And **we can't successfully coach anyone else unless we understand ourselves, what we really value, and what motivates us. We need to understand that great coaching comes with great personal understanding (knowing thyself).**

Most people live their lives by focusing on *WHAT* they have to do instead of *WHY* they do it. The endless tasks continue to mount up, and they wonder why they never feel like they're getting ahead. It feels like they're sprinting on a treadmill just trying to keep up, and every task completed is quickly replaced by new ones. Coaching especially presents these challenges and obstacles.

Great coaches have a great sense of self. They know who they are and *WHY* they are coaching. They know their strengths and understand their weaknesses and strategies for managing both. Life gets a lot simpler and more rewarding when we stop to ask ourselves *WHY* we do things. When we find this *WHY*, we will be given direction and a bigger purpose. Remember that it's not who or what we coach, but rather *WHY* we coach.

When you find your bigger WHY you will be given a clearer direction and a bigger purpose.

You need to ask yourself *why* you love it and why it's important to have it in your life. In my coaching career, I've been doing this exercise over the last three or four years, and I found that my list has become more and more refined as I go. I would say that 10-15 years ago, the things that were most important were winning titles, trophies, and climbing the ranking ladders with my athletes. That was my bigger *why*, but in the last few years I would say that has changed quite a bit, as it's now focused on bettering standards, life skills, and athletic skills. Of course I want to see my athletes succeed on the court, field or track, but to see them succeed later on in life is the gold medal for me. Just like you need to know your athletes' *why*, so do we as coaches.

7 Ways To Stay Motivated:

1. Set Goals.

2. Keep it fun.

3. Keep a Journal.

4. Be Accountable.

5. Grow your passion.

6. Keep a good Attitude.

7. Celebrate the small wins.

3. The 'Energy Business'

In this chapter we have already covered the fact that being a great coach involves these three things:

1. Having the personal energy to perform at a consistent and high level (lifestyle habits and choices).

2. Knowing that your athletes and clients come to you more for your energy and attitude than your exercises.

3. Knowing your *WHY* and what motivates you.

When I meet new people, they sometimes ask me what I do career wise. My answer to them is that I'm in the service and energy business. To which they say: *"Oh, so you are in the electric or solar business?"* It's a corny joke, I know, but as coaches, we really are in the energy business. One thing we need to realize is that we can't be everything to everybody. When I was in my 20s and early 30's, I tried to be everything to everybody. I loved to help people and wanted to be their personal coach, nutritionist, psychologist, house planner, wedding planner, you name it! However, over the last 10 or so years, I have realized that this is just not possible. Sure, I might know quite a bit in the sports performance industry, but it's physically impossible to be juggling all these balls on my own. I can't be everything to everyone. I retain more energy when I pass on some of the responsibility to those who are more qualified in those specific areas. This enables me to concentrate and focus on the areas that I am good at and enjoy.

By delegating the work to people who have more time or are simply better at it than me, it not only allows me to channel my energy into what I love to do, but it shows my athletes that I truly care and want the best for them. I have always believed that if I am not finding the best people for my athletes in the area that they need attention, then I don't have their best interests at heart.

Recently I got in the car and traveled four hours across Florida to meet one of the best S&C professionals in shoulder rehab and strength, Eric Cressey. Eric works with some of the best MLB baseball players in the United States. Right now I have an athlete who is struggling with a recurring shoulder problem, and I wanted to get his opinion and possibly have him see my player. Great coaches are not afraid to lose a client or athlete. They are secure in their abilities and qualities as a coach. They know what they can and can't do. They understand their strengths and weaknesses. **In my opinion, you steal your own energy by trying to be everything to everyone instead of reaching out and finding the best resources for your athletes' problems.**

Find out what it is you really love to do,
and focus your energy there.

Energy Requires an Inner Happiness

You might be able to fake it for a while, but having a great energy is about inner happiness and authenticity. I can recall a coach from Germany who approached me for a consultation during a conference where I was speaking. Katrina and I sat down in the hotel lobby and she told me she'd been in the coaching business for over 20 years, but she felt that she had fallen out of love with it and was afraid she might not rediscover her passion again. I asked Katrina WHY she coached. Then I asked her to list five things she loved about coaching and five things she disliked about it. When she was finished, I began to see why Katrina's passion and love were being sucked out of her. She was coaching all age groups in an academy, kids from 8 to 18 years of age, and didn't enjoy the competitive environment of tournaments and competition. I then asked her what would be the perfect age group and level for her to coach, to which she said kids between 6-10 years of age. I then advised her to focus her energy in coaching kids in that age range and to become the most knowledgeable and experienced coach working with kids between those ages.

She went back to Germany and asked the academy owner if she could solely focus in this area and build the fundamentals group (6-10 years), to which he agreed. A year later I received an email from her thanking me for restoring her energy, passion, and desire to coach again. Katrina had simply lost her way, working with an age group she didn't enjoy that affected her whole inner happiness and love for coaching. Katrina now runs one of the most successful fundamentals kids groups in the South of Germany.

Know Thyself

Today, the coaches who are in the most demand are the ones who have a great energy and make others feel the same. Again, it's that 80/20 principle of having great interpersonal skills.

We also have to understand that we are not always going to have great days and feel like a million dollars, however, this is an area that we need to guard carefully. When we are exhausted from burning the midnight oil and morning coffee machine, we need to make sure feelings don't get in the way of facts. This is when it's good to follow the ancient Greek aphorism of *know thyself.* It's important to know when you need to step away or take a time-out when you are confronted with something that has 'ticked' you off. By not guarding your energy or losing your cool, or saying something you might regret later, it can have a detrimental effect. I know when I begin to get impatient or grouchy, I need a little 'time-out.'

Battery Recharge

Just like your battery runs down on your iPad or phone during the day, so too does your energy level if you are not refueling and taking care of yourself throughout the day. Again, you can't give energy if you don't have it yourself. You might get away with burning the candle from both ends for a few weeks or months, but believe me, it will catch up with you, not only from a physical and health standpoint, but also your spiritual, family, and personal relationships.

You can't give energy if you don't have it yourself.

One thing that I have never excelled at is planning purposeful vacation time. I admit I'm terrible at it! In coaching, and especially working with professional athletes in different sports, there is hardly any down time. When some athletes are having their off-season and downtime, there are others who are in the middle of their busy season. If you are not planning your work structure around yourself and occasionally taking time out, you will most likely burn out. It's important as a coach to plan your breaks and involve your family as much as possible in those plans.

I am getting better at this. In fact, just this past December I took five days off between Christmas and the New Year, where I spent time reading and relaxing. During those five days I was able to finish three books and spend some quality time with family. I was contemplating doing seven marathons in a seven day race, but I didn't feel that that was the 'recovery' I needed, so I settled for doing seven marathons and a half marathon in seven weeks.

Burn-out

Back in 1999 I crashed and burned out badly! I was putting in 10-hour workdays, and my weekends were spent at my athletes' sports events and competitions. On top of that I was training three to four hours a day and racing between 20 to 30 triathlons per year, some in Europe for a professional team I raced for. I thought I was invincible! It was literally night and day how quickly I hit the wall. All of a sudden I started to have flu like symptoms and zero energy to walk from my bedroom to the fridge. At first, I just thought I was being 'lazy' and unmotivated, but in fact, I was seriously ill. I tried to battle through it for a while, but it became so destructive that I couldn't eat. I dropped from 71 kg (156 pounds) to 56 kg (123 pounds) within three months, and basically had to change my whole wardrobe due to my clothes practically falling off me!

At that time I was a personal trainer and had a client who happened to be a doctor from Belgium. She diagnosed me as having a serious immune virus. The years and years of all the training and long hours at work had begun to catch up to me. In a trade-off for training sessions, I received medical care, but it would be about two years before I would feel 'normal' again. After getting back to training, I was struck with another blow. On a flight from Johannesburg to London to complete my final nutrition exams at Middlesex University, I felt my lip and chin begin to swell like a balloon. I had a little scab or piece of dead skin on my lower lip that had been there for a while, but had never thought much of it. I completed my exams with a throbbing lip and an accelerated heart rate from nervousness. The next morning I flew back to Johannesburg to see a specialist and have a biopsy done by Dr. Elliot. It was malignant cancer and it was very serious. It had traveled down my inner chin and was close to my glands. I was told that if it was operated on immediately, I still might only have three months to live! I needed two more operations in the next three years. I am thankful to Dr. Elliot for his exceptional surgical expertise of leaving me with just a light scar on my chin. Hence, the 5 o'clock shadow of stubble you usually see on my face to try and disguise it. Dr. Elliot's son Grant, a great cricketer, actually went on to represent New Zealand and has become a solid batsman and member of their national team. The pot of gold at the end of the rainbow was that just one year later, I won the silver medal in my age group at the World Duathlon Championships in Atlanta. It just shows you, always keep believing you can.

Protect Your Energy

Each day we encounter a wide range of energies, both positive and negative. Like me, you may come across people who either give off an aura of positivity, or the opposite, negativity. I remember standing in the Starbucks line one morning on the way to a practice with a track athlete. There was a woman in front of me who was obviously one negative individual. She was mumbling and grumbling to herself about the length of the line, the girl behind the counter taking forever, and how late she was going to be for work. Her negativity and energy was draining. I was thinking to myself, imagine sharing an office with this woman. Do you know people like this? They are energy vampires and love to suck the energy out of you, pull you into their negativity party. My advice to you is 'get away' and don't get sucked in!

I remember lending a hand with a high school soccer team in Florida a few years ago. This team had two coaches both of whom couldn't always be present at the practices or games. One of the coaches (let's call him 'Jeff' to protect his identity) was a total energy vampire. For example, he would complain about the pitch, the referee, the opponents, and even the weather! The other coach was Graham, more of an upbeat, positive guy who loved being out there and coaching. Well, it's easy to tell who the players enjoyed more and performed better for. When Graham conducted the practices you could feel a different energy and intensity in the players.

Once I learned to protect my energy and be able to **walk away from negative people and situations**, I felt another level of happiness and energy. This is why it's important to choose the right people to have around you. Ever heard the expression, *"You become the five people you spend the most time around?"* — It's so true.

> ### *"You are the average of the five people you spend the most time with."*
>
> *– Jim Rohn*

If there's one thing that I'm very protective of it's my energy space. My energy is incredibly sacred to me. To me success is all about energy. That's why I categorize people into energy givers or energy suckers. Energy givers are those people who you are easily attracted too. I'm not talking about physical appearance, even though that does contribute to a degree. I'm talking about those who make you feel energized and ready to take on the world. Their conversations aren't about themselves. They are deeply interested in you and your well being. **Spend time with these people and they will energize and inspire you.**

Energy suckers are those who simply want to take, take, and take. They complain about everything. They simply suck the life out of you. Where the energy givers see the glass half full, the energy takers want to drink the half full glass and then complain when it's empty. Energy suckers are like leaches. Avoid them. I encourage you to spend time with the energy givers, and then become a great energy giver yourself.

Energy suckers are like leaches. Avoid them.

To continue feeling our best, we must ask ourselves, who gives us energy and who zaps it? It's important to be surrounded by supportive, like-minded people who make us feel strong and able to take on the world. It's equally important to pinpoint the energy vampires, who, whether they intend to or not, steal our hard earned energy.

Gravitate towards the energy givers. I encourage you to take an inventory of people in your life. Divide those into who gives you energy and those who drain you. Specifically identify the energy vampires and begin to evaluate the ones you'd like to limit contact with or eliminate completely. **Build an energy shield around you.** Also, never put yourself down as being "overly sensitive." Sensitivity is an asset as long as you learn how to protect yourself from negative feelings. Understanding how you react energetically in the world is particularly important if you're chronically tired and want to build vitality. Great coaches understand that knowledge is power. Meeting your energy needs can balance mind, body, and spirit to create a vibrant life.

Bring a great energy every day !

Coach Time:

1. *Does your attitude reflect a great energy?*

2. *What changes are you willing to make to acquire more energy in your life?*

3. *What motivates you?*

4. *Do you feel you are consistent in your moods, energy and attitude?*

5. *Do you take time to celebrate the small wins with your athletes?*

6. *Have you found your main reasons WHY you coach? What are they?*

"Success is not to be pursued; it is to be attracted by the person you become."

- Jim Rohn

CHAPTER 5

Interpersonal Skills

"If you don't understand people, you don't understand coaching"

– Allistair McCaw

In this chapter we break it down into the following 3 areas:

1. Your Best Ability is Your Likeability.
2. Know the Person, not just the Athlete.
3. The 5 Cs of Interpersonal Skills.

1. Your Best Ability is Your Likeability.

Let's face it, nobody likes a jerk or wants to work with one. The thing is, no matter how smart, experienced, knowledgeable, or how long your hall of fame client list might be, in the coaching business, you need to be able to get along with others and be able to work in a team environment. When I talk about 'team' in this context, I'm referring to anyone that contributes to improving the performance of the athlete, for example, parents, fellow coaches, athletes, staff members, etc.

The more I'm in this business, the more I have realized that the nicer you are to people, the more successful you will be. I'm not talking about 'false nice' here, I'm talking about being honest, genuine, and friendly — that's all. In fact, it applies even more to life — the nicer you are and easier you are to get along with, the more people are going to like you and want to interact with you. And that is why one of my favorite quotes will always be: *"Your best ability is your likeability."*

Your energy and attitude are what make you attractive.

Your interpersonal skills are the life skills you use every day to communicate and interact with other people, both individually and in groups. We have seen that people who have worked on developing strong interpersonal skills are usually more successful in both their personal and professional lives. This, I believe, is an area not enough coaches focus on or put enough time into. I also believe that this is something closely linked to your standards and the way you operate. When working in a team or group environment it's especially important that you are able to communicate effectively and consistently with fellow coaches, colleagues, athletes, and parents.

Great coaches are interested in others.

Great coaches tend to have a number of key skills and attributes. They are usually great at understanding and relating to people, and they are interested in other people. It's true about the saying: *"Interesting people are more interested,"* meaning that interesting people are curious and love to know more about others and gain a deeper understanding. Great coaches have an invested interest in others. They are always striving to learn and get to know their athletes better.

Great coaches love to bring out the best in people. In the book *Wooden,* author Steve Jamison talks about coach Wooden's approach to getting the best from his players. He says that,

"People want to believe you are sincerely interested in them as persons, not just for what they can do for you. If you don't mean it, they know it." You can't fake it.

Great coaches love to bring out the best in people.

To be a great coach you genuinely want to support and help others get to where they want to be. You also need to love seeing others succeed. Great coaches are not jealous, they love to share ideas and thoughts. They are secure in themselves. They are well connected and keep in regular touch with fellow coaches. These are signs of great interpersonal skills. They have time for younger coaches and love to share knowledge. As they say: *"You should always be nice to those you meet on the way up, because you may well meet them again when you're on the way down!"* We need to stay humble and practice gratitude.

Another factor that I believe to be of importance for a coach or any person, for that matter, is not being too judgmental. I had to work on this myself. In fact, it's still a work in progress. It's about putting aside any preconceived ideas about the person and trying to focus on the coaching process, which allowed me to open up and learn about the individual.

We also need to keep in mind that being liked should not be the main goal of the coach, but rather being well respected. Great coaches simply have an ability to get along with others. They are able to show assertiveness in communicating their standards, values, ideas, beliefs, and feelings.

"Always bring the best version of you."

– Jazz Hervin

In my experience as a coach, one area that coaches put far too much emphasis on is chasing certifications or CEU credits. Of course, gaining the knowledge and wisdom is incredibly important to becoming a great coach, but the most important certification you will ever have is what coach Michael Boyle calls a "CNP." What is a "CNP," you ask? It's a *"Certified Nice Person."* Being a nice person, having good interpersonal skills, and simply getting along with others will probably get you more clients and business than all the educational certificates out there!

> *"Probably your most important certification in coaching is a CNP."*
>
> - Michael Boyle

Great coaches are able to communicate and connect well with their athletes. One thing I've learned in the last couple of years is the process of really listening and understanding others before answering, making an assumption, or making a decision. Great coaches see the importance of working on their communication skills as a vital addition to their personal effectiveness toolbox. So what are the key skills a coach needs to develop?

Here are 10 qualities I believe every great coach has:

1. Great coaches have great listening skills.

In coaching, I believe that listening is one of the most important interpersonal skills to have. Great coaches are great listeners, they don't interrupt or try to get their opinion voiced constantly. They let others finish.

Having asked probably over 100 athletes whilst writing this book, what qualities they look for in a coach, almost all mentioned 'a great listener'. I have found that **the more I keep quiet and let my athletes talk, the more I learn about them and what they feel they need. Great coaches don't listen to respond, but rather to understand.** You will remember I already mentioned earlier in the book about my 80/20 principle when it comes to listening and talking. I aim to listen 80 percent of the time to the athlete and only talk 20 percent. When you talk you are already repeating something you know already, but when you listen, you learn something new. By listening to our athletes, we give ourselves the best chance of helping them progress and improve. Another thing that I have learned is that listening will never get you in trouble!

Great coaches don't listen to respond, but rather to understand.

2. Great Coaches Have Consistency.

Having consistency in your attitude and communication is key to building trust and respect from your athletes. As we discussed in Chapter 4, you can't be hot one day and cold the next. **Great coaches are consistent in their messages and moods**. You also might remember what I said about great coaches being like a DJ on the radio? They don't bring a world of problems with them, but rather have a consistent energy.

Great coaches are also able to control their emotions, especially when results or outcomes don't go the way they would like them to. I have witnessed coaches who are extremely moody and angry when their team or athlete loses. This is not a good trait. Sure, you can be disappointed, but great coaches remember that the 'controllables' such as effort, work ethic, and attitude are the most important things to focus attention on. It's important to stay consistent and not be influenced or driven by things that are not in ones control.

Remember that each day you are broadcasting to your athletes or team how you feel: Either positive or negative energy, apathy or passion, indifference or purpose.

3. Great coaches give accountability.

Accountability is one of the most powerful aspects of coaching. **One of our tasks as coaches is to teach and educate our athletes until they don't need us.** Of course, an athlete will always need a coach or a mentor to help steer and guide them, but great coaches give their athletes accountability and responsibility. When you give an athlete a commitment to do something and they know that they will be held accountable, it drives them forward. As Sir Richard Branson says: ***"Train people well enough so that they can leave, but treat them well enough that they don't want to."*** By giving others accountability, you are sending a message that you trust them with what has been asked of them. Accountability breeds confidence. A great coach is never afraid to lose an athlete or client.

One of our tasks as coaches is to teach and educate our athletes until they don't need us.

4. Great coaches use questioning to explore.

Great coaches use questions to not only help them learn and understand what their athletes are thinking and feeling, but also to allow their athletes to explore the answers for themselves. **Great coaches are not about 'telling,' but rather about opening up their athletes to discover the answers.**

156

World-class coaches hardly ever offer opinions. They ask questions to guide their athlete through the issue. It's called 'learning by discovering.' **When athletes discover the answers for themselves, it empowers them.** When you question for exploration, you reinforce in their minds that you believe in them and that their opinions, knowledge, and experience are worthwhile. You also build their confidence and accountability.

Great coaching is not about leaping to solutions and providing all the answers, but rather allowing the athlete time to explore the problem on their own. Again, continuing to ask questions about the nature of the problem, or what might be a possible solution, is a good way to approach this.

Sometimes when we stand back as coaches and let our athletes discover the answers for themselves, It empowers them.

*When it comes to coaching and communication, I always aim to use the 80/20 rule:
80 percent listening;
20 percent talking.*

5. Great coaches see different perspectives.

There is nothing worse than a coach who is stubborn and believes his or her way is the right way. We have discussed already that as a coach, it's important to have standards and beliefs, but when you become so rigid and stuck to them, it can be a problem. Sometimes that 'old school' mentality can get in the way. Remember that life-long learners are always changing their minds, so that they discover and learn better ways. This is where 'old school' can sometimes get in the way of better. Like they say, the most dangerous phrase in the book is: *"This is the way it's always been done around here."* When it comes to 'old school,' I love the fundamentals, but as we discussed in Chapter 3 ('Adapt'), modes of communication and the generations we are working with change, and so must we.

I can't tell you how many times I see coaches stuck in a certain mindset and perspective. Great coaches are able to listen and explore different perspectives, so that they can make better decisions. **They understand that it's not who's right, but what is right.** I notice that coaches who are stubborn and have to be right are mostly insecure people or just power hungry.

The most dangerous phrase in the book: "This is the way it's always been done around here."

6. Great coaches provide honest and timely feedback.

Great coaches are careful, calculating, and understand the importance of when and how to give feedback. They are always assessing the athlete and how they are feeling to know when it's the right time to offer feedback. Great coaches understand that, even though they might want to get their own view across, the athlete might not be ready to receive that information. **Timing is everything when it comes to providing feedback to the athlete.**

Building great interpersonal skills involves listening, reflecting, questioning, and providing the right feedback. The great coaches also understands that when providing feedback, they should strive to make it clear, relevant, helpful, and positive.

I believe that there are two kinds of feedback. There is positive feedback and then there is information, not criticism. Criticism can often be taken personally, whereas information is taken more constructively. The most important thing about feedback is the trust between athlete and coach. It is more difficult for an athlete to accept feedback, especially when it is not positive from a coach they don't respect or trust.

Timing is everything when it comes to providing feedback to the athlete.

7. Great coaches have patience.

Great coaches have patience. They understand that the journey is long and sometimes an incredibly challenging one. Coaches need patience in working with athletes over the long term. Understanding that each individual is different, and one size does not fit all, they need to be patient in their ability to learn new things, as well as develop new skills. Showing impatience is something that not only shows poor skills in your coaching abilities, but more importantly creates doubt and causes loss of confidence in the athlete.

We understand that all good things take time, and just like developing the athlete, it is the same for the coach. When speaking to coaches at workshops or conferences, I always like to use the *'baking a cake'* theory when I talk about impatience, because when you rush or try speed up the process, it eventually flops!

Great coaches don't set out to be a coach ... they set out to make a difference.

8. Great coaches have emotional control.

First and foremost we need to understand that there is a big difference between being emotional and having emotions. Being emotional is allowing our feelings to take over, and how many times have we seen a coach completely lose it? It's about not having total control of our thoughts, words, or actions. Having emotions is about understanding the other person or situation better. It has more to do with empathy and facts. Displaying anger or frustration can be detrimental to a coach's reputation and image. The great coach knows that it's important to keep both accomplishments and frustrations in perspective. We need to remember that it's only a game at the end of the day, not life or death.

9. Great coaches use their sense of humor.

In chapter 4 we talked about great coaches having a great energy. A big part of that energy is having a great sense of humor, and sometimes being able to laugh at oneself. This quality goes a long way when working with athletes, fellow coaches, and their parents. Just like you and I prefer to be around people with a good sense of humor and energy, so too do our athletes. Remember that **every time you find some humor in a difficult situation, you win.** Having a great sense of humor as a coach is also a great way to make the mundane drill repetitions and the boring part of practice engaging, interesting, and fun.

Kim Clijsters, the former world number 1 in Tennis and a multiple Grand Slam champion, is a coach who brings a great energy and sense of humor to the court. Working alongside Kim back in 2014, I was exposed to her qualities and fun sense of humor. Being a great professional, she knows how to balance the work part and the fun part. When Kim walks into a room, you feel a great energy and aura. She now runs a successful academy in Belgium, with some fantastic coaches and players there. If I ever had a child, I would definitely want them to go there.

Steve Hansen, the All Blacks Rugby World Cup winning coach, is also known for his great sense of humor. This is especially important during the longer tours and dealing with the pressure of playing high-level sports. Players often comment on how much they love their time with him.

Great coaches are also able to make their players feel at ease and relaxed through using humor and fun.

Remember that every time you find some humor in a difficult situation, you win.

10. Great coaches go 'overtime.'

This is a message I usually share with the younger coaches, especially those who have just started in the field: If you want to be a great coach, but don't want to work the early mornings, late evenings, weekends, or public holidays, then you can forget about becoming great. In fact, if you want to climb the ladder in any industry and are not willing to put in the time and effort, you can forget about promotion, a bigger position, or a big raise in salary. **Becoming a great coach is about putting in the extra time, embracing the grind, working hard, and doing what others are**

not willing to do. You cannot cheat the grind and sometimes you cannot pick and choose either. It takes years and years of working in the trenches to become great in this field.

As manager and head coach, Sir Alex Ferguson would be the first to arrive at Manchester United and usually the last to leave. This was the example he gave to all the staff and players at the club, which built a strong culture and standard. Just like great athletes, great coaches do more. **Opportunity lies in doing what others don't like to do**. Embrace the industry and put in the overtime!

> *The best of the best always have this one trait:*
> *the desire to be great.*

2. Know the Person, not Just the Athlete.

I was recently asked at a coaching conference where I was speaking, if I felt technology and computers could one day take over the coaching world. In other words, could there be a possibility that athletes might one day have little need for a coach who is a human being? My answer to that was, *"Never."* Why? - Because as humans, we will always crave face-to-face interaction. You see, coaching is much more than just the data, skills, drills, and programs, it's something much deeper than that. It involves addressing an individual's needs, on and off the field. It is the personal interaction and affection that humans crave more than anything.

Remember that we don't coach a sport, we coach people who play a sport. There's a big difference. We are dealing with human beings, not objects. Computers can't read emotions and what is really going on in the human mind. As we know, each day brings something new to the table.

There are two areas to consider when working with the athlete. As coaches, we need to consider and address the performance area as well as the personal area of the athlete.

A key to successful coaching is being aware of the individual differences in your athletes. There are some coaching tactics that work better on different personality types so it is important to tailor communication and motivation based on specific players' personalities. To achieve this, a coach needs to pay attention to the player's emotions, strengths and weaknesses. Knowing the athlete also involves having empathy for the athlete. Great coaches care deeply about their athletes, and a coach needs to be willing to be a mentor and counselor, as well as a coach.

Great coaches also take the time to get to know the athlete as a person. They take an interest in the athlete's life off the field, gym, court, or track. Coaches who take an interest in the athlete's total life are more trusted and respected than those who don't. As a result, coaches who really care about the athlete as a person find that their athletes are more motivated and work harder.

In fact, it's not just about the athletes or players. Watching a documentary on legendary Football coach Sir Alex Ferguson, former player, Rio Ferdinand mentioned how Sir Alex would know all the parents and families of the players. He also had an incredible quality of remembering all the names of every single staff member, player, and family of the players in the club.

Duke University and USA Gold medal Olympic basketball team coach, Mike Krzyzewski, is also a coach who connects on a personal level more with the families of his players. Often he invites the families to team dinners and road trips. This builds a great level of trust and unity within the team.

Michigan State's head basketball coach is Tom Izzo. Coach Izzo has more than 400 wins to his credit and is known for his high energy and positive demeanor that makes kids want to come play for him. Izzo is a great example of a coach who cares deeply about the person and not just the player. Izzo has always encouraged his players to finish their education, no matter how big their pro prospects are. Education is a top priority in his program. The Spartans scored 995, 1,000 and 985 from 2007-2010 on the Academic Progress Rate. When you think about it, that's saying a lot, considering Ivy League schools are the only ones that generally score perfect. Izzo connected with his players. They knew he had their back. This is an example of a great coach.

Great coaches value the person over the player. They understand that building strong relationships and trust are the most important factors to building a winning team or organization. It always reminds me of one of my favorite quotes in coaching: *"People don't care how much you know until they know how much you care."*

A great coach needs good social skills to be able to get the best from his athletes and team members. When I asked former Liverpool football coach Roy Evans what he felt made a great coach, his answer was that a great coach has great management skills and really cares about his players.

Research your Athletes & Teams.

One thing I do before working with any new clients or athletes is try and find out all there is to know about them. I want to know what their hobbies are, how many siblings they have, where they like to eat out, etc. For example, when I was contacted by Egyptian Ramy Ashour, the former world nr.1 and 3x world champion in squash, to help him prepare for the 2014 World Open in Qatar, I did my homework.

I researched everything! I found out the things he enjoyed doing in his spare time, hobbies he had, his family, his favorite places, and what other sports he enjoyed. Knowing these things before meeting him made it possible to have an immediate connection and conversations other than squash and fitness. I believe that when you are able to start off an athlete-player relationship like this, it improves the chances of success a great deal. Cut a long story short, I'm proud to say that Ramy went on to win the World Title that year.

Another example is Australian tennis player, Bernard Tomic. Bernie loves his fast sports cars and music, so it was easy to connect and chat about those things when traveling together or just relaxing.

Former Canadian ice hockey player and world champion, Delaney Collins is another example. Her main loves are tennis (especially Roger Federer), dogs (beagles), and biking. So when working with DC, it was easy to connect and have similar interests to talk about and share. Oh, and Delaney is also a pretty handy half marathon runner too, so that was another area we could connect in!

You see, great coaching is about taking the pressure and stressful energy away from the athlete. Talking only about things related to the athlete's specific sport does not build a personal connection. I've met coaches like this who seem to never shut up about training and related things to performance when they are with their athletes. It's almost as if they don't have any interests themselves outside of their work. Building connections outside of the field, gym, court, or track is vital to a healthier and more successful partnership. Remember that your athletes want to know that you care about them first as people.

Getting off to a great start when you start with a new athlete or team is critical, that is why building a relationships and connection is so important from day 1. Great coach-athlete relationships are not only built on the court, field or track, but more so off of it too.

Remember that your athletes want to know that you care about them first as people.

3. The Five Cs of Interpersonal Skills

1. Connection

Effective coaching is about connecting with people, inspiring them to do their best, and helping them to grow. Coaching is far from an exact science, it's an art. **One thing you will see all great coaches do is connect before they direct.** Great coaches understand the importance of emotional connection. They understand that to have that athlete truly believe and trust in them, they need to value the person, and not just the athlete. These coaches also have commonalities with their athletes, a shared interest, for example, like playing the guitar or watching their favorite football team.

Great coaches know that a foundation of trust is essential to have a connection. We have seen the impacts that great coaches have on their athletes, like football's Pep Guardiola, Jose Mourinho, NBA Basketball's Greg Popovich, and more recently, just retired former world no. 1 tennis player Lleyton Hewitt. Lleyton, now the Davis Cup captain of Australia, has already had a remarkable impact on the new younger players coming through in Australian tennis. He understands that the connection is the most important factor to gaining the trust and respect of his players. Zinedine Zidane, one of the world's best footballers, said this of Pep Guardiola: *"He inspires me, he always brings a positive atmosphere. He also has a connection with his players and knows how to get the best from them."*

Great coaches know how to connect with those they coach!

2. Communication

The great coaches are great communicators. They say less, but mean more. They also understand that what matters is not what is being said, but rather what is being heard and understood. Great coaches keep communication simple and clear. They don't use elaborate words and terminologies to try to make themselves sound intellectual. They don't give long lectures. Instead, they keep their instructions and information clear and brief.

Legendary basketball coach, John Wooden, was once followed for a whole season so his motivational techniques could be studied. What they found was that Wooden's average "speech" was four sentences and usually never longer than 20 seconds! We also learn in Daniel Coyle's book, *The Talent Code,* that great teachers and coaches give feedback in short, clear spurts that are precise and action-oriented.

Today's generation doesn't receive or respond to information like we did 10 or 15 years ago. They don't want to hear long speeches or lectures. The great coaches understand that simple, brief messages are received best by their athletes. We could almost call it 'Twitter coaching' — no more than 140 characters and to the point!

Great teachers and coaches give feedback in short, clear spurts that are precise and action-oriented.

Great coaches also understand that communication is a two-way street which involves a back and forth dialogue between coach and athlete. It's not just about the coach. They also understand the difference between hearing and listening, because listening is a whole-body process that involves two people who make each other feel truly heard.

Great listening also requires significant eye contact. **Personally, as a coach, I have experienced that the best athletes listen not only with their ears, but their eyes**. It's important to know that effective listening also requires our focused attention.

Let's face it, no one enjoys a long lecture or speech, except for the one who's talking.

Another trait of a great coach is that when giving praise or 'information' (criticism), he does this by shouting praise and whispering information (criticism). Being a USA track and field coach, I remember taking a track session in Amsterdam one evening and sharing the track with a few other coaches and their athletes. The groups ranged from State runners to beginners. I distinctly remember a particular coach shouting abuse at his runner in front of everyone on the track. He might have thought it was building mental toughness or felt it boosted his own ego, but feedback like that in front of a group of people is humiliating for the athlete rather than motivating and character building. This is not a great example of how you build an athletes' mental toughness. Mental toughness is gained through GRIT, challenges and diversity, not screaming abuse at them.

Shout praise in public and whisper criticism in private.

We also need to keep in mind that we communicate and say a lot even without uttering a word. Communication is also in our body language. For example, our posture, a look of disbelief, a disgusted shake of the head, or a smile can communicate quite a bit. Great coaches are aware of their nonverbal communication. In fact, studies show that between 65 and 93 percent of the meaning of a message is conveyed through tone of voice and nonverbal behaviors *(Johnson 2003)*. Thus, in addition to becoming aware of the words you use, it is essential that you become aware of your tone and nonverbal behaviors so that you understand the messages you are sending to athletes. Great coaches know that the way they communicate has a massive influence on their coaching skills, relationships, and interpersonal skills.

3. Compliment

We all love to receive compliments, right? Well, the same applies to your athletes. However, we need to make sure those compliments are sincere and genuine. A coach continually showering his or her athlete with compliments will eventually become a situation where the athlete no longer values the compliment or knows if it's genuine or not. Sincere compliments build trust. Giving compliments also boosts energy and creativity. I have often used this strategy to get my athletes mind off something that might have been distracting them.

Great coaches compliment and magnify their athletes' strengths instead of highlighting and reminding them of their weaknesses.

Great coaches are always looking for opportunities to reward and compliment — factors related to a growth mindset.

Especially near or during competition time, great coaches compliment and remind athletes of their qualities and strengths to build their confidence.

Here's another tip: Compliment others in the first 30 seconds of meeting them. This already opens the channels to being more likeable and approachable.

We need to remember that compliments that are more growth mindset goal-orientated are always better for the athlete. For example, complimenting the process with things like effort, attitude, and work rate, instead of outcomes like winning, hitting an ace, or scoring a goal. Great coaches support, encourage, and admire anyone who is trying to better himself/herself. We need more encouragers. We already have way too many critics in this world.

A great example of this comes from Sir Alex Ferguson's book, *Leading,* where he mentions that he would never tell players that they looked tired, even if he knew they were. Instead, Ferguson would build their confidence by saying something like, *"You're looking strong. Nobody is going to be able to keep pace with you!"*

As coaches we need to focus and maximize the athletes' strengths and manage their weaknesses. Too many coaches are fixated on what the athlete can't do, instead of building the athlete by magnifying their strengths.

4. Care

Great coaches really care. For athletes to give their trust and respect to a coach, they need to know that coach truly cares about them, and not just their results. A great coach understands that what he/she is teaching goes far beyond the Xs & Os. This kind of coach does not just teach the skills and provide the tools necessary for that athlete to perform, but also looks for opportunities where the more important life lessons can be taught, such as mastering hardship, handling and rebounding from failures and setbacks, emotionally dealing with winning and losing, honesty, integrity, etc.

A great coach takes an interest in the individual and keeps track of things going on in his/her life outside of the sport, for example, family, birthdays, or events they may have attended over the weekend. Great coaches also aim to build relationships with the athlete's family. They understand that they play a big part in the bigger picture. For the athlete to function and be happy, we need to address the bigger spectrum of what influences that individual. In Coach Wooden's book he explains that you get better cooperation when you are interested in the athlete's family, not just the players themselves. This brings harmony and productive results. Like Coach Wooden, Coach K mentions in his book, *The Gold Standard,* that he made sure the families of the USA Basketball Team were included in trips, meals, and other activities outside of the players' practices and meeting times.

Great coaches care beyond the Xs & Os, the results and the performances. They care about people, not just the athlete.

A great coach also looks for opportunities where the more important life lessons can be taught, such as mastering hardship, handling and rebounding from failures and setbacks, emotionally dealing with winning and losing, honesty, integrity, etc.

5. Contact

Keeping in regular contact with others is important, not just from a business and client retention perspective, but from a relationship perspective. When an athlete leaves a coach or a club, for example, the coach can become bitter, or take it personally. A great coach wishes others well and understands that if he or she is truly good enough, that athlete will probably come back. I can't think of one coach who retains all his athletes. The fact is, people come and go for various reasons: moving out of town, going to college, playing for a different club, etc. I have experienced this with athletes who have moved on to work with other coaches, or sign with other professional teams. However, by keeping in regular contact, saying "Hi" or wishing them "good luck" for a competition every now and then, they realize that I really do care about them as a people, and not just athletes. I have an invested interest in their progress and well being.

Just last week, I received a lovely message from a former athlete I used to coach called Liz, who now lives in Atlanta. Liz is applying for a sports scholarship to attend a university, and was asking me for advice and the routes she should take. It's these moments I feel most proud of when helping someone else. Keeping in contact with fellow coaches and connections within the industry is important, as well. Sometimes, just a random "Hi' message or email can open so many doors or lead to new athletes or projects.

Great coaches keep in contact with other coaches and people in the industry. They know that by keeping in contact and sharing information, they learn, expand their knowledge, and grow. By keeping in contact with others in the industry, their chances of finding a new venture or applying for a position is much more likely. They nurture and value relationships, as well as care for others.

Great coaches have an invested interest in their athlete's progress and well being.

25 Great Traits to Have to Improve Your Interpersonal Skills:

1.Always go the extra mile. Giving extra effort makes people feel extra good.

2.Build confidence in others. Remember great coaching is about them, not you!

3.Treat people the way you want to be treated. This is the most fundamental rule of being with others.

4.Be sincere in your compliments. It's not something you can fake. Shouting "Good job" all the time isn't sincere.

5.Offer constructive feedback. Never make it personal, so provide feedback positively. Give information, not criticism.

6.Catch people doing things right. Tell them what it was exactly, for example: "I loved your effort out there today" or "Thank you for helping me clean up today after practice."

7.Don't keep score, reminding others of what they've done or what you did.

8.Don't promise what you can't deliver.

9.Bring your best. Give everything you do your best effort. It all matters.

10. Be a problem solver. Become known as a person who has solutions and answers or who knows where to find them.

11. Remember people's names. It makes them feel valued and leaves a great impression.

12. Set high standards and live up to them.

13. When speaking to others, give them your undivided attention. Try to listen without interrupting. Also communicate

appropriately. Adapt your communication to fit the time, place, and person. Think to yourself: "Is this the right time to discuss this with this person?"

14. Make your contribution greater than your reward. Always give a little more than you get.

15. Smile. A smile is an invitation to connect.

16. Compliment the person in the first 30 seconds of the conversation. It will make the person feel valued.

17. Show respect. It's the bottom-line due of every person you meet.

18. Share the credit. When something important has been accomplished, share the credit. Remember, nothing great was ever accomplished alone.

19. Talk with people, not at them. Engage people by truly connecting with them.

20. Stay away from toxicity and toxic people. Help others learn what is toxic in their lives and how to avoid it.

21. Be on time. This shows respect to others and how much you value their time.

22. Help others focus on their strengths, not their weaknesses. The world already has enough critics.

23. Do things without being asked. As long as you know it's appropriate, do something helpful without being asked.

24. Bring a great energy everywhere you go. In all honesty, nobody wants to hear about your problems.

25. Add value constantly. It takes discipline and sacrifice, but it's worth the effort.

'Fix it' Coaches

Something that I often notice in the coaching world is that us coaches just love to 'fix things'. We start with an athlete or team and we just want to jump right in there and fix everything as fast as possible! Our minds are racing with ideas and we think we have all the answers! We want to show the athlete and others just how much we really know. However, **the mistake we make is doing this without first taking the time to build a relationship and better understanding of the team or athlete**. Especially in working with elite or professional level athletes, this can be a huge mistake. **We need to understand and respect that before any change can happen, trust and respect must be present first.**

Let me put it this way, would you completely trust someone and be ready to change things after just 1 week of starting with them?

You cannot force an idea or message on someone who is not yet ready to receive it. We must never underestimate the power of planting a seed first. That's why it's important to first build up a relationship and gain the trust of the athlete or team, before you try and start changing things. **'Fix it' coaches might sometimes have the right ideas and actually have the answers, but to have a 'buy in' from the athlete or team when it comes to changing or introducing something new, there must be first a 'believe in'.**

Before there is a 'buy in' from the athlete,
there must be first a 'believe in'.

In conclusion, we need to remember that the role of the coach is more than just the Xs, Os and the results. We coach people, not a sport. That means we need to build relationships and develop trust. The success of a great coach is found in the personal relationships with each individual he or she coaches or works with. By gaining a greater understanding of the person, by improving the bonds and forging deeper relations, you can have a great influence over that person's future. A great coach is continually working on themselves and their interpersonal skills.

Coaching is not about winning, but rather about changing lives. If we miss that, we miss the point and real purpose. Remember, our interpersonal skills will get us much further than our certificates, knowledge or résumé!

Coaching is not about winning, but rather about changing lives.

Coach Time

1. How much time do you devote to working on your interpersonal skills?

2. What are the areas you feel you could improve on regarding your interpersonal skills?

3. Can you identify your strengths and weaknesses when it comes to your interpersonal skills?

4. Do you go the extra mile for your clients and athletes? If so, how?

5. Do you do some research on your athletes' before you start to work with them?

6. Do you look for opportunities to share life skills and not just performance or game skills with your athletes?

People who want to succeed in a certain area of expertise, surround themselves with people who are better than them. It requires humility, but it will help you be your best.

CHAPTER 6

Fundamentals

"The fundamentals may be boring, but it's where excellence and consistency are created."

- Allistair McCaw

Something I've always found when I talk about the importance of the 'fundamentals' at a workshop or coaches talk, is that there seems to be an attention drop in the interest of what I am saying. In fact, even the word itself doesn't really correlate at all with its first three letters 'fun'. It seems that the fundamentals have a reputation for being dull, boring, and somewhat tedious. The truth is that the fundamentals aren't exactly exciting or have you sitting on the edge of your seat, but one thing for sure is that they are a necessity in mastering any skill and producing world-class results.

All the great coaches I've worked with, observed, or studied, have been great teachers and endorsers of the fundamentals and basics. They just seem to have a deeper relationship, understanding, and respect for them than the rest.

Back in Chapter 2, you might remember that I explained my method and system of working with athletes. I listed the four pillars, namely muscle, movement, motivation, and mindset, to which these are built on the foundation. And that foundation consists of:

1. Standards

2. Preparation

3. Fundamentals

We have already touched on Standards and Preparation, so in this chapter, I'd like to discuss the importance of learning and knowing the fundamentals. I'd also like to show you why they are so vital to developing and mastering skills.

I've divided this chapter into three key areas:

1. The Fundamentals are the Foundations.

2. The Fundamentals are the 'Unnoticeables.'

3. Great Coaches Embrace the Fundamentals.

1. The Fundamentals are the Foundations.

Just like a tall building or structure is built on a solid foundation, so too is a champion athlete, master violinist, or any world-class performer who has mastered a certain set of skills.

A few years back on one of my trips to New York for the US Open, I took the afternoon off and decided to take a cab out to 'Ground Zero,' the site where the fallen Twin Towers and World Trade Center was located. While standing at the remembrance fountains, I was humbled by the magnitude and depth of the foundations. It reminded me how important a deep foundation must be to be able to build such a high structure. The same applies for the athlete, when the foundations of athleticism and game skills are greater, inevitably the chances of success are bigger.

In my experience, after observing many coaches in a variety of sports throughout the years, I have come to realize that the great coaches may have many skills, but the most evident ones are their standards, relationship with the athlete, and their deeper focus on the fundamentals of the game. Along with that observation, the lesser coaches seem to be more easily distracted by other things, like the latest fads and gadgets, instead of building their inter personal skills, as well as their knowledge of the basics and fundamentals of the game.

Sticking to the basics and fundamentals requires patience and discipline.

A common occurrence we find in today's coaching world is that a lot of coaches simply don't stay close to the basics and fundamentals enough. I think there are a few reasons for this. First, I believe that lack of patience is a big reason. Today we live in a world where many seek instant gratification and have a 'results now' mindset and expectation. It seems that everyone is in a rush to produce the next Rory McIlroy, Stephen Curry, Michael Phelps, or Lionel Messi, but are not willing to lay the proper foundations and have the discipline needed to stick to the basics and fundamentals. We need to respect that it takes many years to develop a world-class athlete or performer.

Second, there are many distractions in our high tech world, especially the Internet. I feel it plays a big part in distracting so many coaches away from the fundamentals. Why? - Because we are exposed to a multitude of coaching and instructional websites and sources. We can simply click onto a page, such as YouTube or Facebook, and find a multitude of skills, drills, and exercises. The great coaches are not enticed by the latest fads and never veer away from the straight path. You see, they know what matters and what gets the results.

Part of my method has always been about maintaining those high standards of teaching and adhering to the basics and fundamentals of the game. This doesn't mean I'm not interested in researching and learning every day, but I think the longer you are in this industry, the easier it is to see what is legitimate and what isn't. I think it's easier and more common for the younger coaches to get lured into the technology and scientific aspects.

Part of my method has always been about maintaining those high standards by teaching and adhering to the basics and fundamentals of the game.

During the 2015 Rugby World Cup, I listened to an interview with the All Blacks Fitness coach Nic Gill. Asked how and what the All Blacks did in their training sessions, Nic mentioned that they have no fancy equipment, gadgets, or gyms, they just do the really basic things really well. He spoke about how the All Blacks stuck to the fundamentals and did the simple things consistently. He also mentioned that in New Zealand they had no hi-tech gyms or machines for the players, just the basics they needed and what really mattered. I totally share Nic's views and love the simplicity of it all. We must stay focused on what matters, like the 'need to do' consistent fundamentals and putting in the hard work. We must have the discipline to be able to see through these distractions and stay loyal to what really matters most. Like Nic said, it's nothing fancy, just the simple things done consistently well, everyday.

Nothing fancy, just the basics and simple things done consistently well, every day.

Why are the fundamentals important?

The fundamentals are not difficult to learn, hence the reason they are called *the fundamentals.* Though the fundamentals are simple to understand, it's the daily chore of applying these fundamentals and basics that take patience, effort, and self-discipline. This is where we divide those who reach a high level from those who don't. This is also where the difficulty lies — in being disciplined to the fundamentals. To be successful in something, you need to be attentive to the small details. **Simply put, It's the little things done well and consistently that add up to greater things over time.**

To be successful in something, you need to be attentive to the small details.

In 2015, I attended a US National badminton training camp in Orlando, Florida. What struck me was the attention to detail and how much time they spent on the fundamentals. **There was nothing flashy or 'impressive,' just a focused intensity in the players doing their daily routines and doing them extraordinarily well.** It was almost robotic like, but the focus and purpose of the training was solely on the fundamentals. In one particular drill, the coach had the players seated on the ground and hitting shuttles into a bucket placed on the opposite side of the court. The players had probably around 100 shuttles each, and when they had finished what was in the box, they collected them and started all over again. This must have gone on for around 45 minutes, the same shot over and over. There was no changing the drill to make it more exciting or make everyone happy. It was clear they all understood what would make them better — boring purposeful repetition. Each and every shot was done with precision and purpose, from the take back of the racquet head to the contact and control of the swing. They were locked in and focused, and every so often the coach would give an instruction or comment that wasn't more than two sentences long. The players would simply give a nod of approval and continue working away.

It was almost robotic like, but the focus and purpose of the training was solely on the fundamentals.

Basketball great Michael Jordan credits his accomplishments to the coaches who taught him early in life how to master the fundamentals. Jordan said; *"I had to learn the fundamentals of basketball, because you can have all the physical ability in the world, but you still need to know the fundamentals. I discovered early on that the player who learned the fundamentals of basketball was going to have a much better chance of succeeding and rising through the levels of competition than the player who was content to do things his own way. A player should be interested in learning why things are done a certain way. The reasons behind the teaching often go a long way to helping develop the skill."*

Teaching fundamentals in any sport is critical in maintaining consistency. It's in this consistency where the success and real rewards lie. This is also the foundation for establishing good habits and routines. For example, we might witness a brilliant on-the-run passing shot by Roger Federer, or some brilliance on the squash court from Ramy Ashour, a 3 pointer from NBA's Stephen Curry, or soccer star Ronaldo dribbling to score, but it is imperative that we **emphasize to our youth that learning the basic principles in their respective sport is more important then these moments of brilliance.**

Great athletes are extraordinary because they can do the ordinary things incredibly and consistently well. They make less mistakes, and that, in a nutshell, is the main difference. The same goes for the great coaches as they have built up a consistency and attention to the details, which may not be making headline news, but certainly produces the results!

In my last 22 years or so in coaching, every great coach I have crossed paths with understands and teaches the fundamentals and basics. In fact, they excel at this. I believe that all coaches in a youth sports environment should become acclimated with teaching the fundamentals of their sport. Continuous focus should be placed on having players repeat the basics of their sport. We need to understand that the results, wins, and losses, are secondary to the teaching of fundamentals on the youth level. The rewards are found in having the patience and persistence while mastering the fundamentals.

> *The rewards are found in having the patience and persistence while mastering the fundamentals.*

Great coaches understand that it's important to spend time on the basics and fundamentals. As coaches, we almost need to teach and integrate them into our athletes' DNA, so they can execute them in competition automatically and without hesitation. The quality of your habits under pressure comes down to the attention to detail you have on the basics and fundamentals. **Consequently, under pressure your habits will always come through.** As they say: *"In pressure situations, you don't rise to your level. Instead, you sink to the habits you have created in your practices."* We need to drill, practice, and rehearse the simple things — the simple skills and habits — until they become part of us.

You can always tell an athlete who has been trained well in the fundamentals, someone who has developed great habits and a controlled mindset. The pressure moments in competition reveal these things. It's impossible to reach an elite or world-class level without being world class in the fundamentals.

> *I have never worked with a world-class athlete who wasn't coached well in the fundamentals and basics.*

Scott Evans, the Irish no. 1 badminton player and a two-time Olympian, put it this way: *"The basics and fundamentals are the most important element there is to training. Without them it would be impossible to reach or attain greatness."* Scott understands that he might not have the flair and brilliance of some of the Asian players who dominate the badminton world, but he knows that if he practices and executes the fundamentals and basics consistently well, he puts himself in the best position to succeed.

In pressure situations, you don't rise to your level, instead you sink to the habits you have created in your practices.

I also believe that many coaches today are afraid to stick with the fundamentals due to fear of being seen as 'noncreative' and too simple. Those who understand what it takes to create mastery will understand that these are the traits of being world-class — sticking to the basics and doing them exceptionally well. I like to tell coaches that they shouldn't be surprised if they are criticized for keeping things basic and simple. In fact, I feel complimented when someone observes a training session of mine with an athlete and comments that it wasn't that exciting, or they didn't see anything 'new.' What we tend to often see in youth sports these days is that some coaches feel pressured by parents to change up drills and make it fun for their kids. The parents complain that their kid find the practices boring as they are always doing the same drills and exercises. This is where a great energy and personality of a coach comes in. The great coaches are able to make the boring interesting and fun.

Also, we need to remember that one of our roles as coaches is to educate and explain to parents the development process, fundamentals, and teaching of skills. It's not all going to be fun and games.

The great coaches are able to make the 'boring' more interesting and fun.

The great coaches are disciplined, patient, and invested in the fundamentals. They understand the journey and respect the time it takes to develop and master a skill. This is another area that I feel needs to be addressed and explained well before starting with an athlete, especially to the parents if they are still involved. The biggest issue in developing an athlete is that any talent the child may show, the expectancy of a parent or parents rises and impatience creeps in to the rate of development. In most cases, the parents are gauging the child's results, wins and losses, instead of their skill development as a barometer of progress.

I always tell coaches that they shouldn't be surprised if they are criticized for keeping things basic and simple.

I believe that the most common mistake coaches make when running a youth practice is neglecting the fundamentals. Some coaches are too concerned about how much variety is needed and that the parents are kept happy. I believe that the majority of youth practices should be spent on skill development. The fundamentals should be taught correctly and then practiced using purposeful repetition. I believe that establishing a good foundation with fundamentals should be the primary responsibility of youth coaches.

We must have the discipline to be able to see through all these distractions and stay loyal to what really matters most — the fundamentals.

The Human Factor

Today we see coaches being lured into the world of what I call 'laptop coaching.' These are the coaches who spend the majority of their time looking behind a laptop studying charts, stats and graphs, instead of actually coaching the player or athlete. They can tell them everything from the speed of their racquet or club velocity to the angle of their players left toe! But what they fail to understand is that without the fundamentals of good coaching, instruction, and communication, the player cannot progress.

We need to remember that the human factor (face to face coaching) will always be the most powerful element in coaching. It's all about how the coach interacts with the athlete on a day-to-day basis. This, in my opinion, will always be the number one determining factor for success — and no technology can replace this.

We need to remember that the human factor (face to face interaction) will always be the most powerful element in coaching — and no piece of technology can replace this.

I can't tell you how often I have seen a coach use the term *"train like a pro"* or *"world class athletes use this method,"* but when I research information on this, I find that they haven't trained or even worked close to a world class athlete! In fact, I can guarantee you that a video posted with all the 'fancy', will have triple the number of hits and likes of a video that just has the 'boring' fundamentals.

Boring people

In his TED Talk *Habits of Highly Boring People,* Chris Savve talks about how 'boring' people tend to be more successful in life. He mentions that boredom is not necessarily about people, but more about the way that people do things. In his presentation, Savve tells us that people who are seen as 'boring' are able to stick to repetition and tend to not want to jump to the 'exciting things' as fast. He mentions that these people are usually able to achieve higher levels of success due to their ability to focus and stick to the basics better. This doesn't mean we all need to be boring in order to be successful, it simply means that the outside world will view this kind of trait in a person as 'uninteresting' and 'unexciting.' Attaining any high level of success requires being different to others. So if boring is the worst thing you are labeled as, maybe it's not such a bad thing after all!

One such player that comes to mind is the 6'8" tall South African Kevin Anderson. Kevin reached the top 10 in 2015 for the first time on the ATP World tennis rankings. Having worked with Kevin during that year, I remember standing in the US Open gym speaking to another coach while Kevin was warming up for his match. The coach (who works with a former world no.1 player) asked me how it was going with Kevin and how I was able to work with such a 'boring' guy! My answer to him was that I loved it, to which he looked at me surprised! I went on to tell him that Kevin had such a great focus and attention to the little details. In fact, I liked to compare Kevin to a Formula One driver, someone who loved to know about the whole car and someone who loved to ask *WHY* all the time — not in a disrespectful way, of course, but more in a learning capacity and better understanding. Kevin was fantastic at the basics and fundamentals. In fact, you would have to pull him away from the court because he could mentally handle thousands of reps of the same drill. Kevin's 'boringness' was his strength and toughness. He was able to handle the monotony of repetition and stay locked into the basics. These are the qualities of a champion athlete and world-class performer. Players like Kevin challenged me to be better and I like that.

'Boring' people are able to stick to repetition and tend not to jump to the 'exciting things' so fast.

Throughout my coaching career, I must confess that I've always relished the opportunity to work with older and more experienced coaches — people like SA Volleyball Coach Pete Snyman, Anne Spann, Nick Bollettieri, who is now in his mid-eighties, as well as the legendary cricket World Cup Coach, Bob Woolmer. That's not to say I don't enjoy working with the younger guns, but I always love how much closer and respectful the older generation of coaches are to the fundamentals in coaching. This is where I believe *'Old school is cool.'* The most important lesson that I have learned from working or spending time with these coaches, is that they are extremely patient and excellent at doing the ordinary things extraordinary well. Nothing fancy, but always effective and purposeful.

The fundamentals are the little things that make the big difference — simple things, like a well structured and executed warm-up routine done everyday, or getting in the correct ready position before performing a drill. In fact, I never start a drill with my athletes until they are in the athletic ready stance. These are the simple 'unseen' examples of the little things and basics that the outsiders don't notice. When the little things are done meticulously well, big things happen. We need to learn the fundamentals just like any other skill, through practice and repetition.

When the little things are done meticulously well, big things happen.

2. The Fundamentals are the 'Unnoticeables.'

Here's the thing about the fundamentals: They are usually the foundations that the fans or outside world tend to overlook or hardly even notice — the routines and preparation of a tennis player stepping up to the line to serve, the calming of the mind and control of the breathing; the perfect foot placement; the exact number of ball bounces; the load of the legs and the perfectly timed serve motion. Or a golfer about to tee off with his focus on the target; the foot set up and body position; the feel and hand position on the grip.

Doing these little unforeseen, but critical basic things well, are what make the big differences in the end. In his biography, the late Yogi Berra, who spent most of his playing career with the New York Yankees, explains how important it is to stick to the fundamentals. He said, *"It's all about paying attention to the basics. In baseball it's the fundamentals. You always hear about not sweating the small stuff. Well, some little things they say you shouldn't worry about are more important than the big stuff. It's better to never assume anything. When you master those little skills called the fundamentals, you tilt the playing field in your favor."*

The difference any one fundamental skill makes in your overall performance will be minimal, but when you add those little increments up over time, they give you a huge edge over your opponents. When I asked Tim DiFrancesco, the LA Lakers fitness coach, about Kobe, he said, *"Kobe was so committed to the fundamentals and basics, more than anyone."*

Always pay attention to detail and make a habit of doing the little things better than everyone else.

Having had the privilege to attend many of the professional tennis tournaments, I have witnessed world no. one tennis player Novak Djokovic at his practices. I usually check the practice roster of the players the night before and then plan to go and observe. I love to notice those 'unseen' basics that others might miss. For example, when you observe Novak warm up and prepare for a match, it's methodical and precise. You see, a world class athlete of this magnitude has been taught well in the basics and fundamentals. Like Kobe, he 'gets it'. I love watching these great athletes during practice time, because that is where all the unseen preparation and behind the curtains work happens. That is where you witness the countless repetition and attention to detail, more than in the match or competition. Observing athletes like Novak, reminds me of the iceberg affect, as what you see on the surface (Watching him on TV for example) is not the reality of just how much work and sacrifice has gone into what lies below the surface.

While I'm on the subject of Novak, I just returned from Indian Wells last week and had the opportunity to observe him warm up for his match against Jo Wilfred Tsonga. Novak had 2 trainers there to warm him up, and this process started almost two hours before he played. I counted at least 25 mobility exercises and around 20 flexibility exercises before he went onto the movement and reaction part of his warm-up. This is an example of what it takes to be truly great. Novak has been dominant, especially in the last couple of years during the Rafael Nadal and Roger Federer era.

It's during practice time that you get to witness the countless repetition and attention to detail of the best athletes, more than during competition.

Another athlete I always loved to observe was eight-time world squash champion Nicol David. I had the privilege of working with her for two years and was able to witness her focus and discipline to the fundamentals of the game. Everything was detailed and done with precision. From the way she carefully gripped her racquet to the day she would step up to the box to receive, raising her racquet in the ready position. Everything mattered and it was in these small things, the things that so easily get unnoticed, that she went on to have a successful career, spending almost a decade at the top of the world rankings.

Throughout my years of working closely with champions and Olympians, I have discovered that the athlete who learned the fundamentals extremely well at a young age is going to have a much better chance of succeeding and rising through the levels of competition than the athlete who was content to do things his own way. Winning at a young age with too much competition can impede the development of an athlete.

When working with youth, the goals of a coach should always be to teach sound fundamentals and continually revisit them. Again, this is why I believe it's so important to have a method or system that supports your coaching beliefs — a philosophy that supports how you structure sessions, keeping the fundamentals included in EVERY practice session, and giving your athletes the routines and tools to create great habits.

Something I love doing when I attend a PGA golf tournament is visit the practice putting greens and driving ranges where the professionals warm up. I was invited by my good friend and one of the smartest brains in the world of golf, Mark Immelman, to attend the Arnold Palmer invitational at Bay Hill. Mark is a fantastic coach and commentator for the PGA TV network. On that day I was able to observe Adam Scott, Jason Day, and Justin Rose, among others at the practice driving range. What struck me about these three professionals was their focus and concentration each time they stepped up to the ball. Even though it was just practice, they still went about the details and preparation that they would out on the course during a round. It's evident to see these world-class players were taught well at an early age on the fundamentals, and have developed world-class habits over the years. They understand that IT ALL MATTERS.

The athlete who learned the fundamentals extremely well at a young age is always going to have a much better chance of succeeding.

"I think one of the biggest compliments I can receive from someone who has observed one of my sessions with an athlete, is that it was 'boring' and nothing more than the basics done well."

-Allistair McCaw

Always break it down and simplify.

We already spoke about the reasons why so many coaches have difficulty with sticking to the fundamentals. Yes, they are repetitive, yes they are boring, but therein lies the reason why only a small percentage eventually succeeds and masters them. So many athletes see a huge mountain in front of them, instead of breaking it down to smaller parts or pieces. When we break things down and focus on the fundamentals, we then begin to see things so much clearer and are able to address one thing at a time. By doing this, we gain confidence through achieving smaller goals and progressing through the basics. **Great coaches are more about subtracting than adding. They understand that adding only leads to complexity, whereas subtracting simplifies and keeps things understood.**

You need to break the fundamentals down and keep it simple.

One of my strategies when working with an athlete who is struggling with technique or something in his/her game, is to start simple and break it down to the fundamentals. That means solving the 'obvious' things first. Not only for the athlete, but for me as a coach, it's important to break down the problem into small chunks instead getting overwhelmed by too much information. This has been a successful strategy in solving issues in athletes' games or technical abilities. I always remind them to break it down and simplify. Don't try and learn it all at once, just get through one task and then you can move on to the next. Remember, we need to progress from simple to complex. It's all about getting back to the fundamentals and keeping it simple.

Great coaches will take the time to study the fundamentals.

The Fundamentals are where the 'Magic' Happens.

When people see world-class athletes performing live or on TV, you'll usually hear words like 'talented' or 'gifted.' These are two words that I have a great dislike for. What these people fail to see are the countless hours of repetition and struggle it took for each and every world-class athlete to get there. No great athletes have reached a high level in their sport without tough challenges to overcome. These great athletes didn't just wake up talented, gifted, or even, 'lucky,' as some like to say. They seem to think these athletes are magicians or they've been born that way and somehow got to the top. The truth is, these athletes have been solid in the fundamentals and basics.

Having been around world-class athletes for close on 20 years now, I have not met one who didn't go through tough times and have to deal with things like huge disappointments, injuries, or failures. It is no coincidence that the best athletes you see at the World Cup or the Olympics are where they are for a reason. They have given more and dedicated themselves more than anyone else to be there. They have mastered the fundamentals and basics over and over. They have developed a closer relationship with repetition and the 'boring.'

Are you born or made a great athlete?

I always love listening to debates on this subject. You may totally disagree with me, but in my opinion, I believe you are 20 percent born and 80 percent made of who you become. That 20 percent constitutes your genetics and environment. Being born an endomorph, for example (large boned structure), you won't make a great long distance runner. If you're born an ectomorph, you will probably not be a front row rugby player or NFL linebacker due to your small boned structure and size. Another area to consider is that your parents' influence will decide your environment, where you live, what sports you play, and who will coach you.

The other 80 percent is the work and time you need to put in — the years of sacrifice and time needed to reach the highest level. No matter what the sport may be — kicking, throwing or passing a ball, swinging a bat, club or racquet — you need to master the movement patterns and fundamentals over many years to progress to a high level.

Part of my philosophy has always been about building the athlete before the player — hence, the importance of developing as many athletic skills as possible at a young age, so that the individual has a broader range of skills and ability to withstand more physical stress later. A better athlete will be less likely to get injured and have a better all around game IQ and awareness.

I believe that you are 20 percent born and 80 percent made of who you become.

In my method of training and coaching, almost everything I do stays close to the fundamentals. For example, in our warm-ups, it provides me with a perfect opportunity to monitor how the athletes perform their routines and look to correct basic movements. Anyone who has worked with me will tell you that practice starts as you walk onto the court, field or track, not when the first ball is thrown or hit. With each and every practice I run through a checklist that involves checking on basic running technique, lateral movement, change of direction, acceleration and deceleration skills, as well as body posture.

In all my experience of having worked with world-class athletes, as well as being around other coaches who have done the same, the commonality is that they all mastered the basics and withstood the time and discipline of sticking to them. They were the best at mastering the mundane and handling purposeful repetition. 99 percent of the time they had coaches who were disciplined and loyal to the fundamentals.

Part of my philosophy has always been about building the athlete before the player.

Poor coaching to me has always been a lack of attention to detail and straying away from the fundamentals. What we often see is coaches who get bored with the routine and mundane fundamental drills become impatient and look for something more 'exciting' or 'interesting.'

My philosophy and method focuses more on the constant rehearsal and practice of the fundamentals using simple to complex and slow to fast progressions. However, regardless of the level of the athletes, youth to professional, they still perform the movement patterns of their chosen sport at slow to medium, medium to fast. By doing this, they are in control of their body and are consciously focusing on executing the proper movement skills and control of their body. When an athlete is performing a specific movement with a club, ball, or racquet in hand, I call these 'M.I. Skills.' 'M.I. Skills' stands for 'Movement Imagery Skills.' Through these movement imagery skills, they are able to focus on integrating the technique and movements at a slow speed. The attention to detail and ability to not let standards slip is the key to bigger results.

I have always believed that a great coach understands that the fundamentals of any movement system prime the body for longevity instead of just focusing on short-term performance. Again, the fundamentals may not be sexy, but they sure produce the results.

The attention to detail and ability to not let standards slip is the key to bigger results.

Why do the fundamentals work?

1. They keep it simple.

2. They never change. They are the rock and foundation of a program.

3. They focus on what really matters.

4. They maintain a level of consistency.

5. They break things down and make it easier to learn.

6. They are an essential in creating mastery.

3. Great Coaches Embrace the Fundamentals Better.

There are a few terms getting thrown around in the sports training world these days, and it seems they have become fairly standard. Today we have 'master coaches.' I mean, just what is a master coach? It seems there are already teenagers who have claimed master coaching status!

Another term being overused is 'high performance.' It seems everywhere you look, everyone is running a high performance program or training facility. Again, on closer observation, the majority of these 'high performance' programs are far from anything like high performance. High performance has to do with the standards, the quality of the coaching, and the level of the athlete — day in day out. High performance is all about working with the elite level in a particular age group and athletes who are at the top of their class.

It seems these days everyone runs a high performance program!"

People can easily be misled as to what defines high performance. Many people think that a great coach needs to be on a laptop computer with a high tech software program, or use the latest training gadgets and training tools. This is not what 'high performance' is. I am not condemning them, as they have their purpose, but I find that some coaches hide behind these tools rather than coach. Sir Clive Woodward said recently: *"The single biggest opportunity for delivering a winning performance is through coaching and by really understanding knowledge."*

If you were to ask me what 'high performance' stood for, I would describe it as a program or system that promotes high standards, at the same time developing and training athletes who are already at a high level, and who adhere to the repetition of the fundamentals.

To me 'high performance' is about maintaining the highest standards and working with high level of athletes.

It's futile talking about the small details if the bigger fundamentals are not being addressed. That is like building a house on top of sand and then being more concerned about the color of the paint. When I observe athletic coaches at work, the first thing I look for are basic things like the way their athletes are running in warm-up laps. Do the players have good running techniques? It's the basic mechanics of how an athlete simply runs where it all starts for me, no matter how fast they run a 40-yard sprint or how 'elite' a player is. I have witnessed elite and professional level players who can't run or move efficiently. When I see this, I always think to myself, "Just imagine how good they really could be!"

In my method, I make sure that every single training session I have with an athlete involves the movement rehearsal of the basics — no fancy stuff, just plain old basics. It's useless pulling out all the circus tricks, bullet belts, and harnesses if your athlete doesn't know how to move or even run properly. Great coaches focus and teach what matters, and we need to cover the basics consistently. We need to take care of the big rocks first, then add the pebbles and sand to the jar afterwards.

'High performance' is about high standards, quality coaching, and staying close to the fundamentals. High performance is not about how advanced your sports science or software program is, nor is it about how much fancy training equipment you are able to impress others with. Great coaches stay close to the fundamentals and understand what high performance really is.

Purposeful Repetition and Mastering the Mundane

In Daniel Coyle's book, *The Talent Code,* we learn that the great coaches are able to stick to and teach the fundamentals. He talks about the importance of athletes and great performers in other fields being willing to embrace the repetition and what he calls 'deep practice.' This involves purposeful and deliberate goals and objectives for every practice, with intensity and focus.

In the book, he talks about repetition having a bad reputation, with it being viewed as dull and uninspiring. However, we learn and know that repetition is the single most powerful lever there is to improving our skills. He also talks about high leverage practices and that they share a few common characteristics:

1. They are focused. You aren't pre-creating the entire game, but only targeted situations.

2. They are often untraditional. They don't tend to fall into the list of conventional practice techniques, and as such, are easy to marginalize or overlook.

3. They are habitual. High-leverage skills aren't built in a few specialized sessions; they are built over time, through repetition and routine.

With these things in mind, we see that sticking close to the fundamentals isn't exactly exciting, but is necessary in developing the skills to become great at something. As Coyle explains in his book, the elite performers and great athletes are the best at repetition, they are able to 'master the mundane' and deal with the boredom better.

While working with former world no. 2 and double Grand Slam champion, Svetlana Kuznetsova in 2012, I remember having lunch after a practice session at the Sanchez-Casal Academy. It was another hot Barcelona day in the middle of summer, and it was nice to be out of the sun relaxing in the coolness of the restaurant.

The academy's restaurant overlooks a few of the facility's tennis courts, and on that particular day there was a coach standing out on a distant court wearing a huge sombrero hat. This coach was feeding balls to a young player who was running left to right over and over again. As we chatted over our usual lunch consisting of salad, pasta and chicken, Svetlana said to me: *"Macca, you see that coach there? He does the same two drills every day with his players, and I mean every day! I spent my earlier years training with him while growing up here in the academy, and we would perform the same two drills every day for hours. Backhand-forehand-backhand-forehand, repeat, repeat, repeat. It was tough, but I can tell you this, that repetition and consistency was and is, a big part of the success I've had in my career and game. He taught me that the fundamentals and basics are the most important, and that If I can stick to them, I will be a champion one day."*

It seemed to have worked, because Svetlana has won two Grand Slams and reached a career high number 2 in the world!

Any coach who does not understand that his or her primary responsibility is to create fundamentally sound players doesn't get it.

Malcolm Gladwell's book, *Outliers,* popularized the 10,000-hour rule, which states that it takes 10,000 hours of deliberate practice to become an expert in a particular field. I think what we often miss is that deliberate practice is repetition and revision. If you're not paying close enough attention to repeat and revise, then you're not being deliberate. You see, many athletes put in 10,000 hours, but very few put in 10,000 hours of repetition and revision. The only way to do that is to stay locked in and dedicated to the fundamentals of the game. You can tell the great athletes from the average ones by the way they're dedicated and locked in to the repetition of the basics. The average ones want to continually change up things all the time.

You can tell the great athletes from the average ones by the way they're dedicated and locked in to the repetition of the basics. The average ones want to continually change up things all the time.

Coach Wooden

How can we mention the importance of the fundamentals of coaching without including one of the most famous of all the coaches who endorsed and exemplified the fundamentals — UCLA legendary basketball coach, John Wooden? If you haven't read any of his books, I highly recommend you do. In one of his books, *Wooden on Leadership*, we learn that what really matters the most when it comes to coaching is keeping it as simple as possible. Coach Wooden's approach was always about keeping things easily understood and staying close to the fundamentals of the game. He was all about taking care of the small details for his players. For example, every season started with a lesson on how to put on their socks, because without knowing this, players would increase the risk of developing blisters. Coach Wooden would spend time on these small things while most other coaches would not even bother. He believed that if you focused on the little things that escaped the notice of your opponents and competitors, you would have an advantage.

Wooden believed that if you focused on the little things that escaped the notice of your opponents and competitors, you would have an advantage.

When it came to the implementation of game plans and tactics, coach Wooden's goal was to instill the fundamentals into his players in such a way that they would execute them subconsciously with precision. In his words: *"It is the cumulative effect of doing a lot of little things correctly that eventually makes the big difference in competition. What causes an error or fumble? The answer is found in the fundamentals and attention to detail. Any coach who does not understand that his primary responsibility is to create fundamentally sound players doesn't get it."* His practices were also purposeful and intense, every possibility was addressed that could have been a factor, come game day.

Learn the fundamentals. Master the fundamentals. Teach the fundamentals. Apply the fundamentals.

- Coach Wooden

Back in 2013 I worked with a professional LPGA Golf player in Florida who was coached and mentored by the world famous golf teacher, David Leadbetter. Anyone involved in the sport of golf will recognize the name David Leadbetter, as he's coached players to 19 major championship titles and over 100 individual worldwide tournament victories. Six of those players have even held first place in the official world golf ranking. David is widely known for his fundamental approach to teaching and coaching. With over 45 years of experience in the game, Leadbetter teaches the four fundamentals of his swing philosophy — the grip, plane, release, and tempo. As you can tell like many other great coaches, Leadbetter's success is built on a method, simplicity, and staying close to the fundamentals.

I observed a few lessons of David's, and it always struck me how they were simplistic and basic — no fancy jargon, no funky training aids or gadgets, just good old solid fundamentals and coaching repeated over and over.

In golf we hear about the world's best players going back to their swing coaches, especially when they feel they have lost their feel. The majority of the time, these coaches will help their players go back and revisit the basics and fundamentals to check on their grips, stance, or whatever needs reworking.

It always struck me how his lessons were simplistic and basic — no fancy jargon, no funky training aids or gadgets, just good old solid fundamentals and coaching.

Tom Brady is the quarterback for the New England Patriots NFL team. Brady has won three Superbowls and has thrown more passing yards and touchdowns than any quarterback in NFL postseason history. Every season Brady goes back to his coach,

Tom Martinez, who has coached him since he was 13 years old, to work on his throwing mechanics and fundamentals. Brady, who was the most valuable player in two of the three Superbowls he won with the Patriots, visits his 'go-to guy' Martinez, a 61-year-old former football coach at the College of San Mateo, several times a year for some fine-tuning. Martinez might know more about Brady's technique for passing the football than Brady himself, which is what happens when an all-pro such as Brady completely trusts the coaching he receives from Martinez on fundamentals. *"Tom's a key reason why I've been fortunate to have success in college and the NFL,"* Brady said in a telephone interview. *"I think the world of him professionally and personally. I still consult with him, and he tunes me up when I need him."*

Brady has obviously been doing something right for years, and so has Martinez, in a quiet way, which is the way he wants it. *"I'm a fundamentalist in teaching technique,"* Martinez said. *"It means detail. Even to this day, I consider myself as detailed in technique of quarterback play as anybody I've seen."* Here we see a great example of a world-class athlete and coach who respect and understand the importance of the fundamentals and going back to the basics. Like Kobe, Tom Brady believes in the importance and reward of going back to the basics and doing the repetition.

Another good example of a world-class athlete who revisits the basics and fundamentals of the game to keep his shooting technique in line is NBA Atlanta Hawks Kyle Korver. Korver runs a checklist that includes 20 things (yes, 20 things!) that remind him of all the important elements to shooting correctly. Korver goes back to this list regularly during the season and keeps it with him while playing, often reviewing the list during a game. Korver says: *"I'm not going to check every single one of them every time. There's a certain point, a certain feel I'm trying to get to every day. Some things, you do more naturally. Some things, I have to think about them. As I'm shooting, I have this list in the back of my head, and I know I'm not doing one or two of them. Once I feel I get all 20 of them clicking, then I'm going to have natural rhythm in my shot."*

Remember that this is a player who has probably made over a million throws of the same shot, but is a great example of how important repetition is to an elite athlete.

Korver's mental checklist for every shot he takes:

1. Wide stance.

2. Exaggerated legs.

3. Drop through heels.

4. Engage core.

5. Slight bend at waist.

6. Up strong.

7. Elbow straight.

8. One hand.

9. Fingers spread.

10. Slight pause.

11. Elbow up.

12. Land forward.

13. See the top of the rim.

14. Ball on fingertips.

15. Strong shot.

16. Shoulders forward and relaxed.

17. Ball and arm risen straight.

18. Hold the follow through.

19. Keep the release point high.

20. On turns, square shoulders.

When one embraces and understands the importance of the fundamentals and repetition, great things happen.

Eight Facts about the Fundamentals:

1. Learning the fundamentals takes time, patience and repetitive practice.

2. When we break it down, life is made up of the simple things and fundamentals.

3. Your fundamentals are like your habits. First we make our habits, then our habits make us.

4. Consistency is found in the fundamentals. They may not be flashy, but they get the results!

5. Complexity produces confusion. Simplicity produces clarity and confidence.

6. Learn them, know them, master them, teach them, apply them.

7. The fundamentals are the little things that make a big difference.

8. Break big problems down to the fundamentals.

If I could finish on just one bit of advice when it comes to the fundamentals, it would be this:

Stick to your method and philosophy in times of adversity or challenges. Always return to the fundamentals and basics. This will always be your safe place and 'voice' of reason.

Coach Time

1. *How close do you stay to the fundamentals of your sport?*

2. *How often do you revise and look over them?*

3. *Do you have a checklist of the fundamentals?*

4. *How important do you feel the fundamentals and basics are?*

5. *Do you often explain to your athletes how important these fundamentals are?*

"A great coach is not determined by the level of the athlete he or she works with, but rather by what the coach can do with the level of that athlete."

-Allistair McCaw

CHAPTER 7

Invest

"There is no better investment you can make
than in yourself."

- Warren Buffett

I feel I've saved the best of the seven keys for last. It's also a chapter I had to limit, because I could quite honestly write a whole book on this subject. When I present at coaches conferences, I always love to finish on a high, I aim to send the attendees home pumped and ready to take on the world! It's pretty much the same when I conduct a practice session with my athletes — always finish on a positive, send them home energized, even if they're exhausted!

In my eyes, investing in yourself is the best thing you can possibly do. Why? Because you benefit, and so does everyone else around. Like business mogul and investor Warren Buffett says: *"There is no better investment you can make than in yourself."*

As I have already stated in the previous chapters, there are many commonalities between the most successful coaches and people in the world. But probably the greatest and most impactful one is how much time they invest in themselves and their careers.

You—*yes you*—are your biggest investment. You are the most important place you can put your time, effort and money, and yet you are probably the one who tends to get neglected the most. Why? Because we are in the business of serving of others!

YOU are the most important place you can put your time, effort, and money.

Investing in yourself is not a selfish act. In fact, by helping make your life better, you will, by default, make the lives and performances of everyone else around you better, and isn't that ultimately what our goal is?

Just like the All Blacks state in their 15 principles 'better people make better All Blacks,' so too does it apply to us. A better 'me' makes others around me better too.

Why is investing in yourself so important? Besides being the person you have to spend the most time with, you are also the best example of seeing an immediate return on investment. Unlike other investments out there, investing in yourself is never a risk, because it always pays off. Personally, I have never regretted a day of self-investment. Being a life-long learner has helped me embrace and discover so much more.

Great coaches understand the importance of investing in themselves and their careers. They understand that the payback isn't always immediate, but it always pays off sooner than later.

I've divided this chapter into three main sections, namely:

1. Investing in Yourself

2. Investing in Your Career as a Coach

3. Leaving Your Legacy

1. Investing in Yourself

Investing in yourself is probably one of the best returns on investments you can ever have. Whether it's investing in learning a new skill, developing yourself personally or professionally, it is something that elevates and takes you to even greater heights. It is our responsibility to take the time to develop our god given gifts and talents, so we can best serve others. Successful people invest in themselves all the time. That might sound a little selfish, but it's something they understand will not only help them, but also those around them. Investing in yourself sends a powerful message to yourself, your loved ones, your athletes, and the world.

Investing in yourself sends out a powerful message.

As we know, coaching is about serving others. It's about putting others' needs before our own. A lot of people who are not in the coaching industry don't realize just how tough and demanding our job can be. Unfortunately, there's a price to pay for this. That price can often result in eventual burn-out, illness, and the breakdown of relationships between loved ones. Great coaches invest in themselves. They invest in things like their health, their families, their athletes, their businesses, and their relationships.

Here's something I strongly believe in — the most important appointment of the day is with yourself. That means putting yourself first, doing the things you feel will make you a better coach, partner, parent, co-worker, human being, etc. When you invest in yourself, a world of opportunities opens up for you. And in the business of coaching you sell your services, you must know that no one will invest in you until you invest in yourself first. When you are the best version of yourself, you will be an attraction magnet to others!

The most important appointment of the day is with yourself.

Seven Ways to Invest in Yourself:

1. Health and Wellness

In Chapter 4 we spoke about the importance of having a great energy as a coach. One thing that I have always believed in is that if we are in the health and fitness industry, it's important that we practice what we preach.

I compare our bodies to that of a car. To get the enjoyment and benefits from a car we need to maintain it and take care of it, otherwise it will break down. The same goes for our bodies. Taking care of your health and wellness is probably the greatest investment you can make. Just as coach Magnus Norman mentioned in his blog, we first have to take care of ourselves before we can help others.

Taking care of your health and wellness is probably the greatest investment you can make.

First of all, I believe it's important that you purposely set time aside each day to do some form of exercise or stretching, even just 20 minutes! This needs to become a daily routine. Saying you don't have the time is not good enough, because you do have the time. In fact, saying that you don't have time to work out or exercise is the same as saying that you don't value your health and well-being enough.

Personally, no matter where I am in the world, another country or at home here in the Florida, I always make sure I get 20 minutes of exercise in the morning. It may be stretching, running, or some strength and core work.

I also make an appointment with a chiropractor once a month. I believe that a great energy stems from being aligned and balanced. I also prescribe this for the athletes I work with.

Other forms of investing in yourself include meditation or having a massage, etc. Investing in your health and wellness is an investment you need to make — daily. Like the saying goes: *"Those who don't find time for health and wellness now, will have to make time for illness sooner or later."* Remember that you are a walking advertisement of your brand and company. At least 20 minutes a day, that's all! *NO EXCUSES!*

To be a great coach you need to have a great energy. That energy comes from taking care of yourself and investing in your health.

2. Better Nutritional Habits

Just like I described the body being like a car, so too can you describe the quality of your nutrition to the fuel you put in it. I believe that 80 percent of the way you feel (energy throughout day, mental alertness, etc.) comes down to the nutrition you take in and how well you hydrate yourself.

When it comes to nutrition,
I believe that it comes down to these 3 things:

1. Discipline: Just like having a training plan, so too should you have a nutritional plan. One just has to look to a competitor in a fitness or body building show to see how they structure their eating plans and have a 'cheat day' once a week. This doesn't mean we all have to start living like a fitness model, but we can definitely learn from their discipline and routines. It's also about making the right choices and sticking to them. We all have our weaknesses, for example, I used to have a craving for chocolate after dinner and before bed, but I was able to curb that craving by having a small chocolate protein shake instead. Again, it comes down to making better choices and habits.

2. Habits: Food gives our bodies the energy we need to function. Food is also a part of traditions and culture. This can mean that eating has an emotional component as well. For many people, changing eating habits is very hard. You may have had certain eating habits for so long that you do not realize they are unhealthy. Or, your habits have become part of your daily life, so you do not think much about them. Remember, small steps toward change lead to more success in making long-term changes. Don't try and go from an 'E' nutritional plan to a 'A+' in a week. It is a good idea to limit your focus to no more than two to three goals at one time. Also, take a look at the healthy habits you have and be proud of yourself for having them. Start with something basic like aiming to have a good breakfast, or drinking at least a glass of water every hour. Once you have established this as a daily habit, you can move on to the next. Remember, start with one thing and make it a habit before moving onto the next.

Don't try and go from an 'E' nutritional plan to a 'A+' in a week.

3. Preparation: Just like the body builder or fitness model, taking care of your nutritional needs takes preparation. I make it a habit to do the grocery shopping every Sunday and then prepare my meals for the week. Especially if I'm traveling that particular week, I'll stock up on snacks and things I can travel with. This helps me avoid spending unnecessary money at airports and having limited healthy choices.

While we are on the subject, please get rid of the term *'diet.'* A diet is not a way of living. Diets fail, they don't work! Simply aim to make better choices in your daily eating habits, and make it a way of life, not a chore. Food is for enjoying, not for counting calories!

In the long term diets fail, they don't work! Simply aim to make better choices in your daily eating habits and make it a way of life.

Here are 10 healthy habits of people who care about their nutrition:

1. They stick to the same menu every day.

2. They eat a good breakfast.

3. They drink water throughout the day consistently.

4. They take in protein every four hours.

5. They don't buy 'junk' food. They keep healthy choices in their refrigerators and cabinets.

6. They are picky, especially at restaurants. They want sauces left off or separate.

7. They come prepared with the right foods for the day, work, or travel.

8. They don't eat processed foods.

9. They snack on healthy choices throughout the day.

10. They don't go on diets or follow fads.

3. Develop Winning Daily Routines

I truly believe that success is to be found in our daily routines and habits. One thing that I learned from my personal training days and having some clients that were successful CEOs of Fortune 500 companies, was that they all had daily routines. They all had structure in their day, from sunrise to sunset. A routine is a plan for the flow of your day. I have found the best way to accomplish things and set priorities is to have daily routines, like a set bedtime, wake up time, the same breakfast, leaving the house at the same time every morning, etc. As a coach, it's just as important to have a set routine. This will help with your structure and ability to get more things done.

Side Note: If you get the chance, I highly recommend you take a listen to the *Tim Ferriss* podcast interview of Tony Robbins about his morning routine.

I have found that the most successful people have daily routines.

I have actually designed my own daily routine notepad that I had printed and bound. I make sure that each day I follow my list of things to be done that day and check them off as I go. On my personal notepad, I follow these things each day:

- My top priorities for the day (no more than two or three).
- Things I need to do (errands, phone calls, etc.).
- Appointments and clients I have for the day.
- My 4 x 20s.
- My hydration intake (glass of water per hour).
- My protein intake (15g every four hours)
- My daily vitamin and supplement intake.

By having a daily routine in place, I find I get so much more accomplished. It gives structure to my day. In fact, it's the same when it comes to the athletes I work with. They need to have structure and develop daily routines to their day, too. Part of investing in yourself is having winning routines. Great coaches understand the importance of this.

4. Surround yourself with good people.

The people you choose to be around and spend your time with influence you more than you will ever know. In Chapter 4 we spoke about the energy providers and energy vampires, those who give you energy and those who suck the life out of you. Luckily you can change who is drawn to you and how people interact with you by changing the way you think and feel about *yourself.*

To improve the relationships in your life, you need to improve your self-image first. We all give off a certain energy or aura. To have positive people in your life, you must first be positive about yourself and your life as it is now. Being optimistic gives you a brighter outlook and more gratitude for what you have, and that radiates higher energy, which naturally attracts positive people, circumstances, and events to you. My favorite saying when it comes to this subject is undoubtedly, *"You become the five people you spend most of your time with."*

To have positive people in your life, you must first be positive about yourself and your life as it is now.

5. Take care of your appearance.

When you look good, you feel good. That's why it's important to take care of your personal appearance.

Through your clothes and body language, people already have an opinion about you before you have even said a word. One thing I have always noticed is that great coaches walk with confidence and look the part.

Common mistakes I see coaches and trainers making today is wearing non related work clothes or shoes. You are in the sports and athletic business, so dress like you are! Also wearing vests or hats backwards while working is another no-go area. Also cover up any tattoos and piercings.

Understand that I am not condemning these things, but rather saying that there is a time and place. In coaching you should always look the part and be professional. Remember, it's all about setting standards.

Through your clothes and body language, people already have an opinion about you before you have even said a word.

I put money aside to buy some new shirts and clothes for work every few months. I like to look good and be seen as a professional. This is a big part of my personal standards, as we spoke about in Chapter 1.

Also, we are in an industry that has us perspiring quite a bit, so that's why it's important to smell good and avoid being a 'Coach Onion.' Believe me, your players will thank you. On the lighter side, a few years back, a French Olympian female athlete I was working with gave me the best compliment ever, she told me that I was the best smelling performance coach she'd ever met – I'll take it!

Here's the bottom line: Keep yourself clean and presentable, dress well, and interact positively with others. It takes time, effort, and a little bit of money to pull that off, but if you do, you'll create an overall positive impression of yourself with everyone you interact with, and that positive impression is something very valuable to have.

Taking care of your appearance is a big part of investing in yourself. Great coaches understand this.

6. Work on your social skills.

Something that has become a rarity these days is manners. For example, holding a door for someone, or walking into a room and saying a simple "hello." Great social skills are a must in coaching. We spoke about the fact that the best ability is likeability, and the more I'm in the coaching game, the clearer this becomes. Greet everyone you meet with a handshake, smile, and willingly engage in conversation. Compliment them and make a great impression.

Even if you aren't much of a talker, just smiling and saying a simple "hello" can make all the difference of how people see you. It costs nothing, but can be worth so much. It's one thing I've personally worked on the past couple of years — saying hello to more people more often, even if they are complete strangers.

7. Become a lifelong learner.

We spoke about the importance of becoming a lifelong learner. One of the things about great coaches is that they love telling stories and have a wealth of information. Some of the best coaches I've spent time with are all well-informed and interesting people. They just don't want to talk about their sport or work all the time! I'm sure you can think of a few of those kinds of people who just always want to discuss work or something related to the sport they coach, right?

There's a direct correlation between individuals who strive for growth in their personal lives and those who thrive in their professional lives. This can be accomplished by committing to the concept of lifelong learning. In an ever-changing world, it's more important than ever to stay current, competitive and up-to-date. Lifelong learners are motivated to learn and develop because they want to. It is a deliberate and voluntary act. Lifelong learning can enhance our understanding of the world around us, provide us with better opportunities and improve our quality of life. Athletes love coaches who have great stories. Who doesn't like to hear a great story, right? Lifelong learners have a wider range of interests and skills to offer.

Lifelong learners are motivated to learn and develop because they want to. It is a deliberate and voluntary act.

There are two main reasons for learning throughout life: for personal development and for professional development. These reasons may not necessarily be distinct, as personal development improves your personal growth and professional development enables employment opportunities. Lifelong learning requires self-motivation. You need to feel positive about learning and about your ability to learn.

What is the best way to start? Simple . . . start with just 20 minutes a day of reading up on a particular subject you might be interested in. Maybe you want to learn more about a country you plan to visit in the near future. If you just dedicate 20 minutes a day, that eventually adds up to almost 10 hours a month!

Great coaches are lifelong learners. They understand that it's a great investment in their knowledge and teaching skills. They also love to tell great stories!

Want to know the difference between interesting people and uninteresting people? Interesting people are interested. Uninteresting people aren't.

Kaizen

What is *Kaizen*? Kaizen is the practice of continuous improvement. Kaizen was originally introduced to the West by Masaaki Imai in his book, *Kaizen: The Key to Japan's Competitive Success* in 1986. Kaizen is continuous improvement that is based on certain guiding principles, such as *good processes bring good results* and *working together as a team.*

Great coaches are on a mission to continually improve and better themselves. Much the same as being a life learn longer, they believe in the Kaizen theory. One of the most notable features of Kaizen is that big results come from many small changes accumulated over time. However, this has been misunderstood to mean that Kaizen equals small changes. This is not the case, as little changes consistently done over time lead to massive results.

In Jeff Olson's book, *The Slight Edge,* he talks about the power of making small marginal gains over time. For example, will eating a healthy grilled chicken salad for a week make a big difference in your appearance? Probably not, but will it make a difference in three months or a year's time? You bet it will.

Great coaches believe that there is always room for improvement. They are always evolving and wanting to learn more. Coaches who follow the Kaizen concept are on a quest of continuous improvement. They believe that good is not good enough. They love to improve themselves in every possible way.

Great coaches believe that there is always room for improvement.

Learun'

What is *Learun*?

Learun is a word I came up with one day when I was out on a training run. *Learun* is the word play of 'learning' and 'running.' In training for my marathons, I have logged many hours listening to podcasts on everything from performance training to successful life stories. I especially love to listen to other coaches talk about their work, their experiences, interesting people in the business sector, and those who have impacted the world in a positive way. I feel I get the benefit of both worlds learning while I run. This is another example of being a lifelong learner and killing two birds with one stone. I also feel it's been a great way to eliminate the sometimes boring and monotonous task of logging miles alone. I take my education with me!

You don't always have to be sitting in a quiet room to learn. Learning can take place while you are working out, driving, traveling, waiting at the doctor's, etc. So what are you waiting for? Become a *Learun* coach now!

'Learun' – Learning while you get fit!

M.E.A.T.

Moving on in years, one big area I invest in is my flexibility, mobility, and tissue quality. It's no fun getting out of bed in the morning feeling pain and stiffness. I can no longer hammer back to back work-outs or runs like I used to in my 20s or early 30s, so the older I get, the more important it is for me to stretch, keep the joints loose, and make sure I have good muscle tissue quality. As a coach we sometimes put our bodies through an incredible amount of stress, from twisting and reaching to throwing med balls and lifting heavy weights, etc. So, each morning I perform what I call a MEAT routine, In fact, my athletes do almost exactly the same routine as part of their pre-practice warm-up.

MEAT stands for:

M — Mobility

E — Elastic (Flexibility)

A — And

T — Tissue quality

The 'MEAT' routine involves:

1. Eight minutes spin on bike (raise core body temperature and increase blood flow).

2. Seven minutes dynamic flexibility & hip swings, etc.

3. Five minutes of myofascial release work — foam rolling, roller stick, trigger ball, etc.

I perform this above-mentioned simple 20-minute routine each morning, and it has made all the difference in how I feel. Even after running back-to-back marathons and half marathons for seven weeks, I performed this simple routine each morning without any issues, joint, or muscle pain. I see this as a great investment in my body, because I hope to coach until they have to carry me away!

4 things to stop and ask yourself:

1. Understand that anything worth pursuing is going to take a lot of hard work, pain, and hard choices. Are you willing to do this?

2. One important key to success is self-confidence. An important key to self-confidence is preparation. Are you honestly preparing the best you can?

3. Never drop your standards because it offends someone. In fact, keep raising them.

Have you set your standards?

4. Progress is made by taking steps, sometimes big, sometimes small. The key is to keep taking them! Are you taking these steps every day?

Just like an athlete spends countless hours working on his or her skill set and craft, so too should a coach.

- Allistair McCaw

10 Traits of Successful and Invested People:

1. They get up early.

2. They read a lot.

3. They are always learning.

4. They exercise regularly and eat healthy.

5. They nurture relationships.

6. They are well connected and liked.

7. They express gratitude.

8. They have great habits and follow daily routines.

9. They give others credit.

10. They are always looking for ways to improve.

There's something I do each morning after I wake up, and it involves telling myself that today I want to be G-R-E-A-T! It's a simple routine I need to do in order to stay 'aligned' and balanced in life.

Wake up each day aiming to be GREAT.

G — Gratitude: I give thanks for all I have: my family and health, for example.

R — Reading/Researching: I get my daily reading done.

E — Exercise: My stretch and workout.

A — Attitude check: Do I have the right attitude today?

T — Thoughtfulness: I think about who might need a message or call today that could boost their spirits or lift them up.

2. Investing in Your Career as a Coach

Often I will consult with coaches about personal development and suggest ways on how they can improve their coaching skills. On most occasions I will mention attending conferences or enrolling to study a course. In many cases, they either tell me they can't afford it, or even worse, they don't have the time! They are blinded by how much money they might be spending and forget what they might be learning and one day possibly earning. **I tell these coaches who say they can't afford to invest in themselves that they simply can't afford NOT to!**

Investing in yourself and your business means taking these steps to grow, keep learning, and ultimately make more money. I mean, let's face it, who doesn't want to make more money?

What we need to realize and understand, that by attending a workshop, conference or seminar, there could be that one idea or concept that could potentially help your athletes reach their goal, or even earn you a couple of thousand dollars extra. Investing in yourself and your business is all about making concerted efforts, getting out there and learning.

Even if you only got one thing from reading a book or attending a seminar — then it's been worth it!

Last year I probably spent about $10,000 on self-investment (yes, that much!). This included trips to various sports seminars (even sports I don't necessarily like), athlete development workshops, speaking engagements, books, podcasts, and others. I also traveled to Stockholm, Sweden from the United States to attend a one day speakers workshop, but what I learned there and took with me has benefited me 10 times over! I'm not saying you need to spend that kind of money, but hey, I could have just as easily gone on a great vacation or spent it on something else. I chose to invest in myself and my career.

The more you are active and involved in this field, the harder it becomes to find new ideas that are of great benefit. Again, we are constantly being challenged by all the gimmicks, fads, and 'gurus' out there making a fast buck. But after 22 years, I have started digging deeper and widening my horizons when it comes to learning. I look into different sports, regardless if I like watching them or not, because there are always new things I can learn. I have also looked at other things such as the arts, fashion, and entertainment industries. There is something to be learned everywhere.

In todays world of social media and advanced technology, we are able to reach out and connect with the best of the best in our industries. Growing up, we couldn't do that, having no Internet or social media that makes it so easy today. I would have loved to have been able to purchase a Skype session or have a phone call with a great coach or someone I looked up to in my industry. Today, you can simply get online and make contact with the best out there! But how many coaches do this? Some would rather spend $50-$150 on a night out or on another pair of sneakers instead of having a consultation or attending a workshop. They don't realize the value in spending $20 on a book written by an expert in their field with a lifetime of knowledge and experience.

It's all about choices. Some people will have no problem spending $100 on a night out, but will be hesitant to spend that same amount on investing in themselves.

Each year I aim for the following goals when it comes to my personal growth and investment:

1. I order from Amazon.com and read at least two books per month

2. I attend at least three different sports conferences or seminars (sports I don't necessarily even work in).

3. I aim to try and listen to one podcast per day (I do this either while driving or out running).

4. I aim to watch and learn from as many other sports as possible regardless of what level it may be.

5. I aim to speak to as many coaches as possible and learn from them.

If you don't invest in yourself, then somebody else will get that position or dream job before you do. Invest in yourself. Why? Because you can't afford not too!

You may disagree with me, but I believe that if you are not spending at least an hour a day reading, researching, or listening to podcasts related to self or career development, you aren't serious enough about getting better. The fact of the matter is this: The more you learn, the more you can make others better, and the more you learn the more you can earn. It's important to understand that **education is not an expense, it's an investment.**

Figure out your aperture and then go after it!

An **aperture** is another word for gap or space. When investing in yourself, your aperture is what you need to do to get from where you are right now to where you want to be. Maybe you are starting out as a coach or personal trainer and would one day like to work in developing athletes, or maybe you are a club or academy coach who would love to work with professional level athletes. The aperture between where you are now and where you want to be is what you need to figure out.

How do we get from where we are to where we want to be? The best way to do this is to write at the top of a piece of paper what your ultimate dream or goal is in coaching. From there, work backwards, writing down the steps you need to take to get there.

For example:

•Maybe you need further education.

•Maybe you need to move city or even country to further your career.

- Maybe you need more work experience and intern for example.

- Maybe you need to attend more workshops and seminars to learn the industry better.

- Maybe you need a higher coaching license or certification.

- Maybe you need to work on your social, communication or speaking skills.

"You have to be constantly reinventing yourself and investing in the future".

- Reid Hoffman

You need to see what you are lacking to close the aperture. Is it more coaching skills you need? Maybe it's your social and personality skills, or how about your marketing skills? That's why it's important to make a list and see where you are at this moment and what is needed in order to reach that goal or dream position. Figure out your aperture and then go after it!

12 ways that great coaches invest in their careers.

1. Great coaches attend workshops, conferences, seminars, etc.

Even with all our technology and access to so many ways of learning, I still believe that this is probably one of the best ways to learn and gain knowledge in our industry. Oftentimes coaches will email me when I am putting on a workshop or seminar, asking if there will be a DVD or recording of it. It's impossible to travel around the world to attend every workshop or seminar you'd like to attend, but being present offers so many more learning opportunities. My advice is to try to attend when you can. I have often made a six-hour car trip across the states to attend a half-day workshop. It's called effort!

Make the best effort to personally attend these seminars or workshops.

Understand that by attending, it's not just the message, but the ability to connect with other coaches and people in our industry, to ask questions, and build a network. That is why conferences, workshops, and seminars are so important to attend. By attending these live events, you also have the opportunity and ability to gain hands-on experience.

Seek out those events and conferences you feel you would be able to gain the most knowledge and benefit from. Plan ahead and budget for them. Also to help with costs, have like-minded coaches team up with you to cover travel or accommodation expenses, etc.

2. Great coaches watch and learn from other sports and coaches.

Having been in the coaching game for 22 years now, I feel I have to search and dig deeper to learn more. That is why I love to attend other sports practices and matches and learn. In fact, it doesn't matter what the sport is: netball, gymnastics, soccer, badminton, you name it, we can learn from everyone and anything. Pep Guardiola, football coach of huge teams such as Barcelona and Bayern spends time learning from volleyball coach Julio Velasco.

Eddie Jones, the England rugby coach learns from sports such as field hockey.

By the time this book goes to print, I will have probably attended over 40 games or practices in six different countries, from kids playing 6-A-Side football in a park in London, to NBA basketball in Los Angeles. It all comes down to the same thing — coaching people and performance. Learn from other coaches, no matter what level or age. Remember we can learn from everyone!

Learn from other coaches, no matter what level or age. Remember we can learn from everyone!

3. Great coaches use social media and follow other successful people.

Growing up during a period of no Internet or social media it was difficult to get all the information we are able to get today. Today we have so many ways to gather information on any subject. At the click of a button we can get answers to almost anything we desire. I personally like to use Facebook and Twitter for not only learning from others, but for passing on knowledge as well. I love to share, because what use is it taking it to my grave?

I believe that being on social media today is a must for anyone who wants to get ahead. I have formed some great relationships over the years with people I have met online and through media such as Twitter and Facebook.

I like to follow successful business people, athletes, and coaches from all different sports, as well as interesting pages on general knowledge and facts. I have learned so much using this social media tool.

One bit of advice when using social media — always keep it professional. I see coaches posting all types of pictures non-work related, which isn't a great idea when trying to build a brand or reputation. Separate your personal life (unless it's something positive or inspiring) from your business when using social media, and try not to get involved in discussions about controversial things like politics and religion.

Great coaches love to share what they know.

4. Start a blog.

Blogging is a great way to create a following and share your thoughts with your peers. Don't be concerned about the number of followers you have, that isn't the reason why you blog. Blogging is a great way to learn how to write and archive your articles. I know many authors who have written books who started out simply blogging. If you are good, your following will grow, but like I mentioned, that should not be your main reason for doing it.

5. Great coaches network and are well connected.

I'm sure you have heard of the saying: *"It's not what you know, it's who you know."* This is also true when it comes to the coaching game. To become a great coach not only requires the skills in coaching, but also the skills in leadership and dealing with people. Being connected is a powerful way of getting ahead and getting the jobs and positions you desire.

I remember attending a seminar where Coach Boyle spoke on the subject matter of: *"Do you know, who you don't know?"* What does that mean? It means that you never know where that coach or person who's sitting next to you in the classroom or coaching with you on the field could end up one day. That 'nobody' or stranger next to you that maybe at the moment works with a bunch of kids, could end up one day as the head coach of a professional sports team or organization. That is why it's important to make as many contacts as possible and stay in touch. Even if it's just a phone call or email from time to time to say "congrats" or a simple "How are you?"

Being connected is a powerful way of getting ahead and getting the jobs and positions you desire.

Try to build relationships with as many people as possible. Constantly be figuring out what you can do for other people and what they can do for you. Make lots of friends and make sure those friends are diverse and active. The next time you need an expert or help on a project, you'll have someone you can call.

And while you are making new friends, you should really get to know them: learn their full names and remember details about them. This changes how people see you (into someone who is friendly, earnest, and caring) and leaves a strong impression on the people who interact with you. The ones who you know best and who feel most connected to you will talk about you to others — this is how your personal brand grows stronger.

Great coaches and successful people are well connected. They nurture relationships and understand the importance of forming a network and solid relationships. It all goes back to your energy and the quote: *"The best ability is your likeability."*

6. Ask another coach to come watch and critique a practice session.

This is what I would place in the 'time to get uncomfortable' category. As coaches we are always telling our athletes to get 'uncomfortable.' We encourage them to do the things they don't like to do to get better. What I do from time to time is ask another coach to come observe me during a practice session. I ask him or her to take down notes of what they see, and then over coffee afterwards, let me know what I did well and didn't do so well. This is how I improve. In order to do this, you need to be open to information (criticism). You need to find someone you trust, someone that will tell you what you need to hear and not necessarily want to hear. I often do this for other coaches, too. Sometimes we might even 'cold call,' meaning drop into a session without the other coach knowing and then surprise them afterwards. Of course, you need to have a close relationship with your fellow coaches to be able to pull this off. You can't take it personally, it must be seen as helpful. I find that this has been a great way for me to learn and get better as a coach.

7. Great coaches read a lot.

Reading is one of the best and cheapest ways I've found there is to invest in myself. In conferring with other good coaches and successful people, I have discovered they all read a lot. In fact, I'd like to stop and congratulate you, because you are on your way to greatness as you are reading right now!

Successful people are reading instead of watching TV or playing X-box. I'm not saying there's anything wrong with watching TV, as personally I love watching sports and a good movie, but lying in front of the TV watching anything for the sake of it, I find is unproductive.

Reading is a great way to learn about so many things. Through books we can open our world and learn about how to do so many things. **Here's another thing I believe, that if I only get one new idea from a book, then that book has been worth every cent.** Call me old fashioned, but I still love the feel of holding an actual book with pages in my hand instead of having a Kindle. Great coaches have a library of great books, In fact I take pride in the fact that I had to exchange my book cabinet for a bigger one earlier this year!

Great coaches read. Poor coaches watch TV.
Great coaches love to share information. Poor coaches hoard.
Great coaches research. Poor coaches feel they know it all already.

8. Listen to podcasts and audio books.

If you had asked me five years ago what a podcast was, I would have had no idea. Listening to podcasts has been a great educational source for my coaching career and me. Being on the go quite a bit, I have found podcasts a great way to learn from different people and industries. I always make sure I download some good podcasts on my iPod before traveling somewhere, and usually end up listening to them in the car or airplane. I also love to listen to podcasts while I run, especially in training for marathons (*Learun*). In fact, just this past Sunday I ran a trail marathon north of Tampa and almost completed the whole audio book of the *Gold Standard* by Mike Krzyzewski.

3 Advantages of listening to podcasts:

1. Podcasts put you in control of your influences. Like it or not, you are influenced greatly by what you hear. Choose to be influenced by people who are already at the level of success you want to be. Success is contagious.

2. Podcasts are free and convenient. I've never paid anything for any of the podcasts I listen to and they are available to me whenever and wherever I want to hear them.

3. Podcasts promote self-development. Similar to reason number 1, a lot of my self-development activities originated with ideas learned through the podcasts I listen to. I love listening to successful coaches and people share their tips on how they became successful and how they are continuing in their success.

9. Coach Another Sport.

Here's another one of those 'time to get uncomfortable' situations. By learning another sport, you challenge yourself to get away from your comfort zone and push yourself to learn and adapt to something else. Learning another sport and learning the culture is never easy, but it opens you up to learning and discovering so much more.

A few years back I decided to coach u/8 soccer at a club in Bradenton, Florida. This decision made me more nervous than training any other Olympian or world champion athlete! It completely challenged me and made me uncomfortable. But it was a gratifying and worthwhile experience, and one I recommend to any coach.

Coaching a local u/8 soccer team made me more nervous than training any Olympian or World Champion athlete I'd ever worked with!

Coaching another sport also helps you learn and get back to the fundamentals of a sport. Just as we discussed in Chapter 6, it's so beneficial to learn and stick to the fundamentals, no matter what sport we are working with.

Just like watching another sport or coach, working in another sport other than your chosen one expands your horizons and enables you to learn more and be more.

10. Watch and listen to interviews.

I love listening and watching other coaches being interviewed. It doesn't matter what sport it may be, but I always love listening to their comments and insights. By listening to interviews, we get an insight into their mindsets, philosophies, and how they approach important games. Watching documentaries and interviews of successful people also helps us learn what mistakes they made, how they got there, and what advice they have for others. Instead of turning off the TV when the match or game is over, listen to what the coaches have to say—and learn!

11. Great coaches keep a journal.

Great coaches keep journals and they write everything down. It has always astonished me that coaches can attend a seminar or conference and be empty handed, meaning they aren't taking notes! This is something I especially tell young coaches: *"Write everything down, EVERYTHING! In fact, if your fingers aren't cramping, you're not writing enough down!"*

Something I always tell young coaches: "Write everything down, EVERYTHING! In fact, if your fingers aren't cramping, you're not writing enough down!"

I have three journals: one for all my training sessions with every athlete I work with recorded; one for new exercises or drills that I think might be of benefit; and another journal for writing down quotes and things I've learned that could help me as a coach. I have three full boxes of old journals from athletes I've trained from the past 15 or so years. I think it's a habit I developed early in my triathlon and running days, as I have 12 years of training log books with every single day's distance, time, heart rate, route I took, and weight recorded.

When asked about Jose Mourinho, the former coach of Chelsea and Real Madrid, Sir Bobby Robson, the head coach of young Jose during his early years at Barcelona, said this: *"Jose listened to every word, he asked questions, he focused intently on what was going on around him and he wrote everything down."*

Great coaches write everything down. They use this for revision as well as reference. They know they can't remember everything they've heard or seen.

12. Set lunch or coffee dates.

There's a saying I really love: *"If you don't ask, you don't get."* This is applicable to what this next piece of advice is all about. Most coaches are willing to give up some of their time to sit down and have a chat with you or set up a Skype call. A great way of investing in your coaching career and learning more is asking a coach to coffee or lunch. This is a great time to connect and ask the questions you'd love to know the answers to. What's the worse answer you can receive? A simple "No." Then my advice is move on to the next one. Keep knocking on the doors until they open.

I try to donate at least an hour a week to help younger coaches, especially those who are starting out and can't afford to pay for a consultation. I actually made time to Skype just this morning with a young coach from Canada. I love to help. It feels good to help others and give back! It energizes you!

Exercise.
Network.
Get up early.
Stay focused.
Read more books.
Practice gratitude.
Write things down.
Listen to more podcasts.
Work harder than anyone you know.

Build and invest in your own personal brand.

A 'personal brand' is in many ways synonymous with your reputation. It refers to the way other people see you as a business owner or representative of an idea, organization, or activity. Are you a genius? An expert? Are you trustworthy? What do you represent? What do you stand for? What ideas and notions pop up as soon as someone hears your name?

When you have a personal brand, people recognize and care about your name, what you're working on, what you offer, and what you're about. Nike brands itself as an expert in creating quality and fashionable sportswear. Jamie Oliver is an expert on food, Dr. Oz is an expert on medical advice. Even if you're not interested in marketing your advice, you need to create the perception that you are very good at what you do.

Continue learning and updating your knowledge, especially if your expertise is based around the online world. The web changes drastically from month to month. If you were an expert two years ago but have since stopped learning and challenging yourself, you're not an expert anymore.

Don't Be a Blinker Coach

A blinker coach is someone who only watches, listens, attends, or associates with things related to the sport they specifically coach and work in. As we know, racehorses sometimes wear blinkers to block their own view of other horses, so don't become a blinker.

The longer I am in this business, the harder I need to look to find and gain new knowledge. A blinker coach doesn't see the value in learning from others sports, other coaches, or even other industries. As I mentioned earlier in the book, I have also studied the arts and entertainment world to see how successful people think and operate. I love watching other sports and coaches, it doesn't matter what it is, because there is always something new to learn. You can find me observing just about any sport from gymnastics to water polo, rugby to Ice hockey, it doesn't matter what it is. I love to absorb the whole gamut!

As I mentioned earlier, Pep Guardiola, learns from his good friend and volleyball coach, Julio Velasco. Eddie Jones, the England Rugby coach, learns from women's field hockey! I have personally learned from sports like cricket and transferred skills and drills into my baseball, squash, or tennis programs. I also learn from watching the pre- and post-game interviews of coaches. This is a great way to learn more and grow as a coach.

A blinker coach loses so many opportunities to learn and grow from other fields and sports. Don't become a blinker coach. Pull your head out of the sand, get out there and learn more from seeing more!

Put just as much time into developing the craft of coaching as you would expect your athletes to devote the same amount of time into learning from you.

Invest in others.

In my opinion, any job or task that involves service or investing in others' lives is very powerful. As coaches, we hold powerful positions having been given the opportunity to influence and better peoples' lives every day, through something we love to do — a sport. Great coaches not only invest in their players from an athletic point of view, but they invest in them from a life point of view. A great coach is someone who can instill great values and lessons into the hearts of young athletes and one day see them be a success in their lives, regardless of what career path they may choose.

Coach John Wooden is a good example of a coach who invested in his players' lives. An interview on ESPN with Bill Walton, the former UCLA player who was coached by Wooden, mentioned that with Coach Wooden, you just knew he cared so much for his players as people. He always wanted to know how things were going at home and how your family and friends were.

Successful coaches surround themselves with good, smart people who challenge them and help them grow. Alex Ferguson had Brian Kidd as one of his assistants; Graham Henry had Wayne Smith and Steve Hansen; Bill Walsh had George Seifert; and Liverpool's Coach Jurgen Klopp relies on long time assistant coach Zeljko Buvac.

As San Francisco 49ers head Coach Bill Walsh said: "Successful coaches realize that winning teams are not run by single individuals who dominate the scene and reduce the rest of the group to marionettes." Great coaches understand they need to surround themselves with great people.

Investing in others is paramount to the success of the team as a whole. That involves spending time and effort training and mentoring those around you.

Great coaches surround themselves with
great people and support.

3. Leaving Your Legacy

We all will leave a legacy, so let me ask you this question: What legacy will you leave one day when you hang up the clipboard, whistle, and stopwatch? How would you like to be remembered, not just as a coach, but more importantly as a person? These are important questions, because in coaching, like life, we need to know what our destination is.

I am so blessed and grateful to be able to coach and work with athletes young and old, which makes me feel like I have the best job in the world. We get to influence people's lives and what could be more powerful than that?

What kind of coach do you want to be? How do you want to be remembered? Take a moment to think of the legacy you want to leave, and how you can embody those qualities now.

Coaches have the ability to make a difference in the lives of those they coach as much as any profession in the world. The difference you make will be significant and permanent, and this all depends on what you choose to put into it. Few professions allow you to have an impact on the lives of people who need you as much as ours does, and that goes for any coach, anywhere.

Your athletes might not remember the scores, the results, or the exercises and drills. They might not remember what you always said, but they will most certainly know how you made them feel. For me, there is nothing more gratifying or rewarding than having a past athlete call me up or send me a message years after I have worked with them to ask for a bit of advice, or just to say, "How are you, coach?" Believe me, this is worth more than all the accolades, trophies, and awards. It's great to know I've had an influence on others' lives, not just their athletic careers.

The fact is you will leave a legacy when you stop coaching. The question is: what will that legacy be?

Don't wait until it's too late to decide what kind of legacy you wish to leave. In fact, take a moment to consider how you would be remembered by the athletes you've coached, if it all ended today. Every athlete who plays or has played for you will somewhat remember their experiences with you. Especially in players' younger years, the potential to make a lasting impact is seemingly endless. Remember, your athletes might not remember what you said, but they will definitely remember how you made them feel!

Take Action Now

It's time to take action. It's time to be the best you can be. It's time to be the example and bring your very best. Act now, because the time will never be just right.

Become your best, and they will too.

Set Your STANDARDS.
Build Your METHOD.
ADAPT to Those You Coach.
Bring a Great ENERGY Always.
Improve Your INTERPERSONAL SKILLS.
Stay Close to the FUNDAMENTALS.
INVEST in Yourself Everyday.

CHAPTER 8

What Coaching Isn't

1. Coaching is not...
Something you do, it's something you are.

2. Coaching is not...
A 'punch the time clock' job. It has no set hours.

3. Coaching is not...
About egos, personal glory or agendas. It's about serving others.

4. Coaching is not...
A job you get into with the sole focus of making loads of money.
It's more about outcomes rather than income.

5. Coaching is not...
About what's best for you. It's about what's best for the athletes
and team.

6. Coaching is not...
All about the championships and silverware, it's about 'people care.'

7. Coaching is not...
All about the Xs & Os, it's about the Ps & Ss (people and
standards).

8. Coaching is not...
About the destination, it's about the journey and lessons learned
along the way.

9. Coaching is not...
About you, it's about others and those you coach.

10. Coaching is not...
A job, it's a vocation and calling.

"Coaching is not all about the Xs & Os, it's about the Ps & Ss (People and Standards)."

- Allistair McCaw

CHAPTER 9

50 things I've Learned as a Coach

At the end of each year, I write down what I have learned. Every year I get to add a few more things to my list. I feel this is a great exercise and way to reflect and grow as a coach and a person. I encourage you to do the same.

I've learned that...

1. You can learn from anyone and everyone, regardless of their age, experience, or status.

2. Your ears will never get you in trouble, so become a better listener than a talker.

3. People don't care how much you know, until they know how much you care.

4. It's critical to look, learn, and take notes (keep a journal).

5. It's important to look outside your sport or area of interest for new and fresh ideas.

6. Truth is, nobody wants to hear about all your problems, so don't bring them to work with you.

7. Your mistakes and failures will teach you your greatest lessons.

8. You shouldn't be afraid to ask for help from others.

9. Keeping it as simple as possible is always the best answer.

10. It's good to stay hungry and humble.

11. There are no set 'hours' in this business. Be prepared to pay your dues, put in the long hours, and work harder than the next person.

12. Coaching is not about the Xs and Os (exercises, drills, sets, reps). It's more about people and standards.

13. It's best to just be nice to people (yes, even if you don't like them!).

14. It's not about you.

15. You learn so much more by watching and learning from other coaches and trainers, not just what to do, but what NOT to do.

16. You don't pursue success, you attract it by the person you become. Your attitude and work ethic will get you much further than your qualifications or education.

17. It's important to communicate well and often. Don't leave things 'unfinished.'

18. It's important to always look professional and presentable. Take pride in your appearance. Have neat clothes, hair, clean shoes, etc.

19. Always come prepared. Get to the practice or meeting at least 10 minutes before your client/athlete does.

20. Try to give some attention to the siblings of the star athlete in the family, the ones who often get ignored and tag along with their star brother or sister to all the practices and competitions.

21. The key to better relationships is in trying to understand the other person better, not just offering your point of view.

22. It's wise to try and stay connected to past athletes. Do not take offense if they leave you. Stay in contact, even if it's just a text every few months to say, 'Hi,' or, 'How are you?" Believe me, if you are good enough, they will come back (or speak highly of you).

23. Be hungry, keep looking for ways to get better. Enroll for courses, listen to podcasts, order a book a month on Amazon, etc.

24. Don't speak ill of other coaches or programs. Try keep these things to yourself.

25. Your people skills will get you further than your exercises or knowledge will.

26. Coaching should be a vocation, not a profession. If it's not your passion, then maybe it's not for you.

27. Learn and practice gratitude.

28. Invest in yourself — every day.

29. Enjoy the journey. Every day isn't going to be great, but keep looking for the great in every day.

30. You are never going to please everyone. You are not going to be liked by everyone. Not everyone will agree with your views, methods, or philosophies. They don't have to. That's life. That's cool. Accept it.

31. Expect to be criticized when you keep things simple. At first they'll think you're not smart, then they'll realize you actually are.

32. Stay off forums that provoke, ignore negative or nasty comments, and avoid arguing a point. If you feel the urge to write something, then make it positive or productive.

33. Treat everyone the same, regardless of their status.

34. The best reward in coaching is having a former athlete tell you that you helped him/her become a respectable and responsible adult.

35. The fundamentals will always prevail. Stay close to them, know them, and apply them.

36. It takes years to become an overnight success.

37. There are two kinds of people. Those who watch TV and those who read.

38. You need energy in order to give it. Take care of yourself. Exercise and stretch daily.

39. It all starts with your standards. Your success and level of results are related to this.

40. Everyone has brilliant ideas, but very few are willing to persist and put the work and time into them.

41. The more you fail the closer you come to success.

42. You should spend your energy on things you CAN control, and don't worry about things you can't control.

43. Success is to be found in doing the uncomfortable and the 'not so pleasant things' — doing what others are not prepared to do.

44. We are all different. So with that in mind, I've learned to adapt to different people and understand them better.

45. Being a teacher, trainer, or coach is a special privilege. We get to influence and change lives. What could be better?

46. I've learned that what got me to this level will rarely get me to the next level. I need to keep evolving.

47. I've learned that when you magnify others peoples strengths; you bring out the best in them (and yourself).

48. The higher you climb the ladder, the more people there are to criticize, pull, or bring you down. My advice is to keep climbing and stay focused on what lies ahead.

49. I've learned that the best example for my athletes and clients is my own example. Not always easy, but I have to practice what I preach if I expect others to follow my lead.

50. I've learned that the more I know, the more I realize I don't know.

Like one of these 50 things?
Then Tweet it by adding the hashtag:
#mccawmethodbook

The best monitoring system and tracker in coaching? A coach who pays attention.

CHAPTER 10

40 Mistakes Coaches Make

They …

1. Sometimes talk too much.

2. Don't communicate consistently and clearly enough.

3. Neglect the fundamentals and basics.

4.Don't ask for advice enough.

5. Try be everything to everyone.

6.Don't invest in themselves enough.

7.Don't take the time to really listen to the athlete.

8.Think that only winning is a sign of progress.

9. Bring and share their life problems to work.

10. Give too much information (information overload) and don't keep it simple enough.

11. Speak on their phones during a practice session.

12. Don't adjust or adapt to a group they are working with (age, level, etc.).

13. Run practices that aren't purposeful enough.

14. Miss opportunities to teach life skills.

15. Try to 'jump in' and correct every mistake.

16. Have practices that aren't fun enough, especially with youth.

17. Don't follow a structure.

18. Lack emphasis on forming relationships with players.

19. Don't teach athletes how to win or lose with dignity and class.

20. Don't spend enough time educating athletes on the 'little things.'

21. Do 'useless' fitness drills that aren't appropriate to developing the athlete or player for that particular sport.

22. Give players all of the answers instead of letting them figure it out for themselves.

23. Lecture and give long speeches.

24. Speak in a monotone.

25. Don't have enough games included in practices.

26. Don't make an effort to connect with the athlete.

27. Use too much sarcasm as a form of humor.

28. Create an environment where kids fear 'getting it wrong.'

29. Don't keep practices flowing.

30. Stop to talk to parents while practice is still going.

31. Focus too much time on the better kids or athletes.

32. Arrive late to practice.

33. Conduct lengthy team meetings.

34. Copy and use drills of professional athletes or coaches.

35. Don't know their *WHYs*.

36. Try to do too much in one practice session and end up achieving little.

37. Don't catch athletes doing the right things often enough and compliment them.

38. Believe and follow all the latest gimmicks, fads and Internet gurus.

39. Don't stick to the LTAD (Long Term Athlete Development) plan and design practices according to age and what is needed in those stages.

40. Don't consistently communicate with parents.

The human factor:

How the coach interacts with the athlete on a day-to-day basis will always be the number one determining factor for success.

No amount of technology can or will replace this.

CHAPTER 11

What Makes a Great Coach

I asked some world-class athletes and coaches to list their three top things they feel make a great coach:

Roy Evans: *Former Liverpool FC head coach*

1. A great coach must have great management skills.

2. He/she must have a good knowledge of the sport.

3. Must have the ability to make decisions.

Trevor Immelman: *Winner of the 2008 Masters Golf Tournament (beating Tiger Woods by three shots)*

It goes without saying that the best coaches are able to take in all information regarding training and technique before deciding what is applicable or illusionary.

1. A coach needs to be comfortable at NOT being the star.

2. A great coach understands how to use an athlete's idiosyncrasies to their advantage so that the athlete can stay as authentic as possible with regard to training, technique, and competition.

3. A great coach has a keen instinct for when to be stern and when to nurture.

Gregor Townsend: *Former Scotland Rugby International and head coach of the Glasgow Warriors*

1. First you must have a love for the job!

2. You should continue to be thrilled by the sport you love no matter how many hours of work you put in. This love for your job will drive you to learn.

3. Finally, the aspect you must love the most about the role is seeing your athletes develop and achieve success.

Angus Mugford: *MLB Toronto Blue Jays mental coach*

1. A growth mindset (the best coaches continue to learn and stay curious and open-minded).

2. They love to empower others.

3. Great coaches realize it's not about themselves, but how they drive growth in others. They demand excellence (they set the bar high and challenge people to strive for more than perhaps they think they are capable of).

Ramy Ashour: *3x World Squash champion and former world no. 1*

1. A great coach must be inspirational.

2. A great coach must understand the athlete.

3. A great coach must have a positive and great mindset.

Gemma Bonner: *Liverpool Football Club ladies captain and England International*

1. Respect — This is probably the biggest thing, having mutual respect will make players eager to learn and apply the coaches' principles, and the coaches will trust the players to do their jobs.

2. Approachable — having a good rapport with the coach is important. Players should not be afraid or intimidated to ask

questions or speak to their coach, knowing they will get honest feedback.

3. Application of knowledge — many people can have good knowledge of the game, but to be able to apply it to coaching and improving players is a key skill. How coaches portray their ideas/coaching points can have a huge influence on the player/team performance.

Darcy Norman: *AS Roma Football fitness coach*

1. A great coach has humility. He or she understands that all egos must be left at the door.

2. A great coach is honest with his/her athletes. He/she tells them the things they need to hear.

3. A great coach must have good character.

Gabe Sanders: *Stanford University track & field coach*

1. Empathy: Gaining an understanding of individuals' personal backgrounds, personalities, and context of their lives is invaluable in building productive, positive relationships between you and the athletes and within a team/program.

2. Embracing Failure: Knowing that moments of failure are not end points, but parts of the journey that lead into assessment and progress in life, professionally, personally, and practically.

3. Passion: Passion of learning, passion of people, passion of growth, passion of everything within the realm of your sport, even with its shortcomings and what can be done to make it better.

Patrick Mouratoglou: *Coach of tennis champion Serena Williams*

1. A great coach is a great communicator. Someone who knows his player well enough to know in every situation what is the best way to have him/her be motivated to do what you want him/her to do, the way you want her/him to do.

2. A Great coach is a generalist, like a doctor. He has to know well enough about technical, tactics, mental, physical, and medical in order to be a good leader of the team.

3. A great coach is someone who has a vision. When he looks at his player, he sees the future player he wants him/her to become and is able to make him/her make the necessary evolutions in order to make him/her achieve his/her goals.

Nick Levett: *Talent Identification Manager at The FA (English Football)*

1. Be humble. Recognize that it's about the players and their development, not about your own ego.

2. Be authentic. Use practices that look like the 'real' game and focus on learning.

3. Be patient. Recognize that player development is a long-term game with no shortcuts.

Tim DiFrancesco: *S & C Coach of the NBA Los Angeles Lakers*

1. Listen: Your athletes want to feel valued and heard. When you make specific efforts to listen to them they feel like you care. It's easy to work for someone who you know cares.

2. Collaborate: When you regularly make your athletes feel like they're part of the training process, they'll buy in at a deeper level.

3. Learn: Your athletes trust and assume that you're staying up-to-date on the latest evidence and information. It's up to you to follow through with this and look to advance your knowledge whenever/however possible.

Sven Groeneveld: *World Class Tennis Coach of numerous Grand Slam Champions*

1. Great coaches are always listening to their students.

2. A great coach gets to know the person behind the player.

3. A great coach is always looking to improve learn and grow.

Nick Winkelman: *Head of Performance at Irish Rugby*

1. Coaches must be EMPATHETIC. The best coaches know how to emotionally relate to their athletes, place themselves in their athletes' shoes, and auto-regulate their coaching to meet their athletes where they are at physically and mentally.

2. Coaches must be great COMMUNICATORS. Communication is not what is said, rather, it is what is heard. We cannot be effective coaches unless we are effective communicators, as communication is the bridge between our thoughts and the athletes' movement and emotions.

3. Coaches must be ADAPTABLE/RESILIENT. Just like we need to be flexible communicators, we also need to be flexible in our operations and programming. Humans are not fixed, rather, they are highly variable and not everyone responds to the same stimulus in the same way. Thus, we need to have a flexible system that accounts for variability within the athlete and have the protocols/solutions to respond accordingly.

David Joyce: *Head of performance at GWS Giants*

1. A great coach must be able to develop and nourish relationships.

2. A great coach must have attention to detail.

3. A great coach must have great communication skills and adapt to the athlete.

Kim Clijsters: *Grand Slam Champion and former world no. 1 in tennis*

1. There must be a Connection.

2. There must be Discipline.

3. Probably the most important one is Trust.

Svetlana Bolshakova: *Belgian Olympic long jumper*

1. A great coach is always respectful.

2. A great coach has great communication skills.

3. A great coach is consistent with the athlete, through the good days and the bad days.

Bradley Hindle: *Malta National Squash Coach & former PSA Tour professional*

1. A great coach always puts the athlete first.

2. A great coach maximizes his students athletic potential and belief.

3. A great coach communicates well and is a great motivator.

Patrick McEnroe: *Former USA Davis Cup captain and ESPN commentator*

1. A great coach must be a great listener.

2. A great coach is able to guide and lead his or her athletes.

3. A great coach inspires others to become great.

Michael Beale: *Liverpool FC u/21 coach*

1. The top coaches are able to simplify what they want from the players.

2. A great coach invests in his/her athletes/team.

3. They go the extra miles to connect with them.

Amanda Sobhy: *USA Squash National Team, World ranked Top 10 and Future World number 1!!!!!!)*

1. Communication: Able to develop a two-way communication street where a coach can provide feedback and advice, but also listen to the needs/feelings of the athlete. A relationship should develop where an athlete should feel comfortable talking to a coach, both on and off the court.

2. Adaptability/flexibility: A great coach does not force the player to only do things one way, but is able to adapt and be flexible to individual differences and preferences.

3. Ability to challenge their athletes to continuously do better and work hard, as well as get athletes to push beyond their limits and also believe in their capabilities.

Juergen Grobler: *British Olympic Rowing coach*

1. People skills in managing young people/athletes and other people around them.

2. Good scientific background and a vision about how your sport might develop.

3. A great coach deals with stress well.

Jack Green: *Olympic 400m runner and European u/23 Champion*

1. A great coach is knowledgeable in the sport they are coaching.

2. There must be trust and him or her must have a great personality.

3. They must care as much as I do.

Scott Evans: *Irish no. 1 and Olympian badminton player*

1. Positivity and good energy.

2. Knowledge (always wants to learn more).

3. A great coach is motivating and inspiring.

Jillion Potter: *USA Rugby Sevens Eagles and Olympian*

1. A great coach has emotional intelligence

2. A great coach teaches values and life lessons.

3. A great coach is strong on the fundamentals and has a passion for the game.

Brian Lynch: *Head coach at Limburg Utd Basketball, Belgium*

1. A great coach has passion. This is something you cannot fake. It ignites your players!

2. A great coach has compassion. It's important to understand what type of player you have and know how to get the most out of them.

3. A great coach is authentic. Don't try to be something else. Be who you are and give everything you got to your players. By doing this, you automatically get all the respect back!

Jason Lee: *Olympic hockey player and coach*

1. They have a long-term plan and vision.

2. They are adaptable.

3. They are not ego-driven.

Nick Matthew OBE: *3 x World Squash Champion*

1. A great coach teaches life skills, not just game skills.

2. A great coach is a great listener and communicator.

3. A great coach recognises the individual needs of the player.

Daniel Guzman: *Head of Strength & Conditioning at LA Galaxy Soccer*

1. A great coach is a life long learner.

2. A great coach communicates well.

3. A great coach is committed to integrity regardless of circumstances.

"As coaches, our job is to make the complex simple.
The simpler you can make it for somebody, the easier it is to do."

\- Steve Hansen

CHAPTER 12

What Coaches Make

The dinner guests were sitting around the table discussing life. One man, a CEO, tried to explain the problem with college athletics. He argued, "What's a kid going to learn from someone who decided his best option in life was to be a coach?"

He reminded the other dinner guests what they say about coaches: "Those who can't play, are those who coach." To stress his point he said to another guest, "You're a coach, be honest. What do you make?"

Having a reputation for honesty and frankness, the guest replied, (at this, Coach Ridder was FIRED up and getting after it!)

"You want to know what I make? I make kids work harder than they ever thought they could. I make a C+ feel like a winner of the Congressional Medal of Honor. I make kids run through 90 minutes of practice and sweat. I make kids turn dreams into reality. You want to know what I make? I make kids wonder. I make them question. I make them criticize. I make them apologize and mean it. I make them cooperate. I make them competitive and respectful. I make them show all their work in front of hostile crowds and perfect their acts of sportsmanship. I make them understand that if you have the will to follow your dreams, should anybody try to judge you by a mistake you made, you must pay no attention, because you tried and gave it your all."

"I make teams from individuals who work together to build success." He paused and continued.

"You want to know what I make? I MAKE A DIFFERENCE, I MAKE LEADERS, I MAKE OTHER PROFESSIONS POSSIBLE." Then he asked the CEO, "What do you make?"

Coaches, the next time you are unhappy with your job because you think you are not making enough money, ask yourself,

"Are you putting the intangibles you make above your bank account?"

I sure hope so...

- Anon

A great coach is always looking for the teachable moments.

CHAPTER 13

10 Tips on Working with Today's Generation of Athletes.

1. Find out how to connect with your athletes. Show an interest in them and find out what makes them tick, what motivates them. Remember, you need to connect before you can direct.

2. Set your standards (rules and conditions) from day one. Make them clear and well understood. Be strict, but fair and stay flexible in certain situations.

3. Embrace social media and technology. This is how today's generation communicates and socializes. Learn to speak their language. For example, today's generation loves to use text and use WhatsApp for messaging.

4. Today's generation wants to know the *WHY* behind everything. So make sure you explain this well. Remember that this generation doesn't need us for information, as they are able to get that at the touch of a button.

5. A 'do I as say' mentality and way of coaching will only work against you. Today's generation prefers a more diplomatic approach. They don't react well when being told what to do.

6. Stay consistent with *everything* you do. Players won't respect you if you don't.

7. Coach attitude and effort before Xs and Os. Without proper attitude and effort, the Xs and Os don't matter.

8. Stay on top of keeping a tight ship. Keep standards and discipline high. You're either coaching it or you are allowing it to happen. You either accept it or correct it.

9. Give accountability. They like this, as it makes them feel important and in charge of their destiny.

10. Develop a growth mindset. Reward effort and attitude, not only outcomes and results. Teach and show them what really matters and how hard work and a great attitude will get them further in life.

Your attitude, standards, and work ethic will get you further than your qualifications or education.

CHAPTER 14

Some Advice for Young Coaches

People who want to succeed in a certain area of expertise surround themselves with people who are better than them. It requires humility and humbleness, but believe me, it will help you to be your best.

If you are lucky enough to find a great mentor, then make sure you offer something back. Don't just be a leech and suck everything you can get, make sure you give back, like assisting that mentor in practices or helping in any way possible. It must be a win-win situation. Believe me, there is nothing worse than having an intern or person who wants to learn from you, but not offer help or assistance back in some way or another.

I want to share with you a few things that every young coach should take on board when it comes to pursuing a career in coaching:

1. Never go to your first interview for a job and ask how much you are going to get paid, or if you get weekends or holidays off.

2. Never complain about the long hours or having to work the early mornings or late evenings.

3. Look professional and presentable at all times.

4. If you don't know the answer to something, go and find out the answer.

5. Earn your stripes. You don't start in the Army as the sergeant major. You start in the trenches and work your way up the ranks.

6. Check your ego at the door.

7. All the qualifications in the world won't make you a great coach. There's a difference between being 'knowledgeable' and being able to bring that knowledge across to those you train in the most effective and most understood way.

8. Keep a journal. Write everything down. Don't think you'll remember it all.

9. Say '*hello*' and be nice to people — yes, it's that simple.

10. Look, listen, learn, and keep asking questions.

11. The world owes you nothing, so don't walk around thinking it does.

12. You will have to work for free, volunteer, and do internships. Don't complain. Instead, be grateful for the opportunities you are given.

13. Learn to handle rejection, but never let it defeat you.

14. Respect those who have gone before you. Even if you think you might know more than them.

15. Keep educating yourself. Read, listen to podcasts, enroll for courses, etc.

16. Never be afraid to fail, because failure is your greatest teacher.

17. Stay humble.

18. Be early, rather on time.

Connect with Allistair

Allistair's goal (plus drive and passion) has always been a simple one: To make those around him even better. A big part of his philosophy is geared around individual self-investment and continuous life learning. Besides training champions, Allistair loves to speak and has presented in over 25 countries worldwide. Some of the topics he loves to speak on include *athlete motivation, building successful team cultures and coaching environments.*

Based in Florida, Allistair consults and works closely together with athletes, teams, schools, colleges, coaches, business professionals and sports organizations.

Interested in having Allistair consult, present, or speak at your organization or next event?

You can contact him at:

Enquiries: mccawmethod@gmail.com

Facebook: McCaw Method

*Twitter: @allistairmccaw Hashtag on twitter:
#mccawmethodbook*

Online: www.mccawmethod.com

Send your comments and feedback to mccawmethod@gmail.com and also don't forget to tweet your favorite quotes from this book on Twitter: *#mccawmethodbook*

"You are stronger, smarter, and more resilient than you think. You are capable of achieving far more than you believe.
You were meant for greatness — like all of those who have achieved it. But it takes persistence. It takes determination. It takes facing your fears and doing that which is hard and necessary, instead of what is quick and easy. It takes skipping the mythical shortcuts and using your imagination as a map and preview of life's coming attractions."

- Zero Dean

About the author

Allistair McCaw is an internationally recognized leader in the field of athletic performance enhancement. His well-proven method of athlete training, *'The McCaw Method,'* has set the standard for providing world-class athletes and coaches with cutting-edge training and knowledge.

A highly motivated and sought after coach in athlete development, Allistair has worked with a host of world class athletes including Olympians, 11 Grand Slam Champions, 3 world number 1 Tennis players, 3 world number 1 & world champion Squash players, PGA Golf Tour winners, as well as International Soccer, Hockey, Badminton, Basketball, Rugby and Cricket players.

He holds various qualifications in the sports performance field, and is a certified USA Track & Field coach, Tennis coach, USA Youth Basketball coach, Golf fitness coach and ISSA Performance specialist.

Allistair is also a highly sought after keynote speaker and has regularly appeared on national television in the United States.

He is a former 5x world championship Duathlete (*run-bike-run*) competitor and 2x national fitness champion, as well as a USA Champion in his age group in both the Powerman Duathlon (2013) and USA Half Marathon beach championships (2016).

Voted in 2015 as one of the top 50 most influential coaches by Coachseek, Allistair regularly contributes articles to various magazines on performance enhancement training, motivation and mindset. He is based in Tampa, Florida.

Notes

MINDSET PREPARATION MOTIVATION

CHAMPION MINDED

An Athlete's Guide to Achieving Excellence in Sports and Life

ALLISTAIR McCAW
JENNY W. ROBB

ALLISTAIR McCAW
KEYNOTE INTERNATIONAL SPEAKER
AUTHOR · COACH

Available on **www.AllistairMcCaw.com** and **amazon**

MCCAWMETHOD
SPORTS PERFORMANCE TRAINING

Made in the USA
Lexington, KY
10 April 2018